WRITERS AND THEIR WORK

ISOBEL ARMSTRONG
General Editor

JANET FRAME

JANET FRAME

Claire Bazin

© Copyright 2011 Claire Bazin

First published in 2011 by Northcote House Publishers Ltd, Horndon House, Horndon, Tavistock, Devon, PL19 9NQ, United Kingdom.
Tel: +44 (0) 1822 810066 Fax: +44 (0) 1822 810034.

All rights reserved. No part of this work may be reproduced or stored in an information retrieval system (other than short extracts for the purposes of review) without the express permission of the Publishers given in writing.

British Library Cataloguing-in-Publication Data
A catalogue record for this book is available from the British Library

ISBN 978 0 7463 1171 4 hardcover
ISBN 978 0 7463 1011 3 paperback

Typeset by PDQ Typesetting, Newcastle-under-Lyme
Printed and bound in the United Kingdom

For Robert, with all my love

Contents

Acknowledgements	ix
Biographical Outline	x
Abbreviations and References	xii
1. Introduction	1
2. Autobiographical Novels	6
3. 'The House of Fiction'	28
4. Short Stories and Poems: Generic Variety	65
5. *An Angel at My Table*	88
Notes	111
Select Bibliography	118
Index	122

Acknowledgements

I am deeply grateful to Mark Greengrass and Emily Eells for their invaluable help. I should also like to thank Alice Braun for her constant support and stimulating knowledge of Janet Frame. I thank Valérie Baisnée for making her chapter on Frame's poetry available to me.

Without the sabbatical semester granted to me by my university, I would not have been able to complete this book. Finally, I would like to thank Janet Frame herself for all she has given me.

Biographical Outline

1924	Birth of Janet Paterson Frame, on 28 August 1924, Dunedin, third of five children of George Frame, a railway worker, and Lottie Godfrey.
1930	The family settles in Oamaru.
1937	Death of elder sister Myrtle by drowning (because of congenital heart defect).
1942	Attends Waitaki Girls High School and matriculates in 1942.
1943–4	Teachers' training college, followed by a brief period of teaching.
1945	First stays in psychiatric hospitals after abruptly walking out of the classroom.
1946	'University Entrance' published in *The New Zealand Listener*.
1947	Death of second sister Isabel by drowning.
1951	Publication of *The Lagoon*.
1954	Final release from hospital. Life at Frank Sargeson's hut in Takapuna.
1957	Publication of *Owls Do Cry*.
1956	Life in Ibiza and Andorra. Meeting Parlette.
1956–61	Life in London. Diagnosis of schizophrenia rejected at the Maudsley Hospital.
1961	Publication of *Faces in the Water*.
1962	Publication of *The Edge of the Alphabet*.
1963	Publication of *Scented Gardens for the Blind* and *The Reservoir*.
1963	Father's death.
1964	Awarded the Scholarship in Letters (New Zealand) for this year.
1965	Publication of *The Adaptable Man*. Awarded the Burns Fellowship at Otago University.

1966	Publication of *A State of Siege*.
1968	Publication of *The Rainbirds*; published in the US under the title *Yellow Flowers in the Antipodean Room*.
1967–1969–1971	Travels to Europe, the US. Takes up fellowships at the Yaddo Foundation (a writers' colony in Saratoga Springs) and the Mc Dowell Colony, Peterborough, New Hampshire.
1967	Publication of *The Pocket Mirror*.
1969	Literary Fund Award.
1969	Publication of *Mona Minim and The Smell of the Sun*.
1970	Publication of *Intensive Care*.
1972	Publication of *Daughter Buffalo*.
1972	Moves to the Whangaparaoa Peninsula (north of Auckland).
1974	Awarded the Menton Fellowship (later to be called the Katherine Mansfield Memorial Fellowship) and works a few months in Menton.
1975	Returns to Auckland.
1979	Publication of *Living in the Maniototo*.
1983–85	Publication of the three volumes of the Autobiography: *To The Is-Land, An Angel at My Table* and *The Envoy from Mirror City*.
1983	Publication of the collection of short stories *You Are Now Entering the Human Heart*. Appointed a CBE (Commander, Order of the British Empire).
1984	Awarded the inaugural Turnovsky Prize for Outstanding Achievement in the Arts. Awarded the Sargeson Fellowship at the University of Auckland.
1989	Publication of *The Carpathians* which wins the Commonwealth Writers Prize for Best Book.
1990	Appointed an ONZ (Member, Order of New Zealand).
2003	New Zealand Prime Minister's Award for Literary Achievement.
2004	Dies of leukemia in Dunedin.

Abbreviations and References

To The Is-Land, An Angel at My Table, The Envoy from Mirror City: I'll refer to the three volumes as I, II, III. I used the three volumes which were all published in 1987 by Paladin. For the sake of clarity I refer to them by systematically mentioning the number of the volume, which appears in capitals before the page number.

AM	*The Adaptable Man*
Ca	*The Carpathians*
DB	*Daughter Buffalo*
EA	*The Edge of the Alphabet*
FW	*Faces in the Water*
GB	*The Goosebath*
HH	*You Are Now Entering the Human Heart*
IC	*Intensive Care*
La	*The Lagoon and Other Stories*
LM	*Living in the Maniototo*
MM	*Mona Minim and the Smell of the Sun*
MU	Marc Delrez, *Manifold Utopia: The Novels of Janet Frame* (Rodopi: 2002)
ODC	*Owls Do Cry*
PM	*The Pocket Mirror*
Ra	*The Rainbirds*
Re	*The Reservoir*
SF	Gina Mercer, *Janet Frame: Subversive Fictions* (Dunedin: University of Otago Press, 1994)
SGB	*Scented Gardens for the Blind*
SoS	*A State of Siege*
TAS	*Towards Another Summer*
WA	Michael King, *Wrestling With The Angel: a life of Janet Frame* (Harmondsworth: Penguin, 2000)

1

Introduction

Janet Frame, one of the most famous New Zealand writers of her time, died in January 2004. It is significant that what won her international fame is essentially her Autobiography published as a trilogy twenty years before and made into the famous Jane Campion film *An Angel at My Table* in 1990. A number of critics, Gina Mercer[1] among them, tend to consider the Autobiography as a far less interesting production than the more innovative, sophisticated, post-modern fiction. Theirs is not, however, an opinion that I share, and it is a work that I think needs re-evaluating. I will defend the Autobiography on the grounds that though it has none of the sophistication of the novels, it is also far more readable. Which is perhaps the reason why some critics find it less interesting. It remains to be decided whether readability is a valid criterion for critical evaluation. Marc Delrez repeatedly speaks of the feeling of unfamiliarity, even of destabilization, the reader experiences on reading her fiction. And though such destabilization can be challenging, it also risks putting the reader off because it resists our interpretation, or even sometimes repels our understanding.

Like most writers, Frame did not write the Autobiography until she was about 60, as the writing of one's life requires a retrospective look upon the past, one that logically can only happen quite late. The interest of studying all Frame's work is that it illustrates the theory of the French specialist of the genre, Philippe Lejeune,[2] according to which the writer of an autobiography does not simply write an 'official' autobiography but inscribes all his/her works in what he convincingly calls an autobiographical space, which may corroborate Frame's own belief that there is no more 'pure' fiction than there is 'pure' autobiography – 'and so the memories do not arrange themselves to be observed and written about, they whirl, propelled by a force beneath, with different memories rising to the surface at different times and thus denying the existence of a "pure" autobiography' (I 161). It is just another manner of working on the same matter. And she goes on to illustrate this apparent paradox in all her works: her novels, short stories, poems, autobiographical novels and the Autobiography itself all bear an autobiographical stamp that is of course most obvious in the 'official' autobiography or in the two autobiographical novels, *Owls Do Cry* and *Faces in the Water*, the latter two inviting the reader to find for himself/herself what is 'missing' in the elliptical autobiographical narrative. Michael King quotes the New Zealand poet Fleur Adcock about Frame's works: 'Her fictional and autobiographical writings are so closely interrelated that to read one work creates an appetite for the others' (*WA* 465). This constant movement, or interpenetration between autobiography and fiction produces what Jean-Pierre Miraux calls a stereographic effect whereby the texts echo each other.[3]

Frame's life-story is indeed extra-ordinary, one that is certainly worth the telling since she spent eight years in various psychiatric hospitals after having been (wrongly) diagnosed with schizophrenia. This experience is first-rate material for the narration of an exceptional life. She writes to make reality bearable but needs an unbearable reality in order to write. It is thanks to the publication of *The Lagoon*, her first collection of short stories that she escaped a lobotomy, still the medical panacea in New Zealand in the 1950s. It is no wonder, as Frame herself declared, that she should have devoted her life to literature as literature had saved it. She wrote before and after being 'mad'.[4]

Frame's story is exceptional, but not only on this account. Frame is a post-colonial female writer and even if (or maybe, because) the question of her post-coloniality has not been frequently raised, it needs addressing, be it only to conclude that she cannot/should not be classified either as a post-colonial or feminist writer, simply because she blatantly refuses and eludes any form of classification. This does not mean that she has no interest in such questions, but that they are always closely related to 'the personal'. It is quite significant for example that in most critical studies on post-colonial literature,

Frame is very rarely mentioned.

In the course of her autobiographical trilogy, she resorts to the following eloquent metaphor: 'On the rim of the farthest circle' (II 117) in her attempt at self-definition. This metaphor could actually be taken at its face value: New Zealand (at least from a European perspective) is indeed on the farthest circle, a sentiment emphasized when Janet Frame undertakes her first trip to 'the continent' (or 'home' as her father proudly and surprisingly calls Great Britain). Her dilemma, her story, is reflected in her country's history: like New Zealand, she is just as distant, equally 'on the rim' of more than one circle. When World War II broke out, it looked more like a farce for the Frame children than a threatening reality. They mimicked Hitler and his 'raving delivery', 'the Nazi salute and the goose-stepping armies' (I 137). The treatment inflicted on the Jews is, however, fictionalized in *Intensive Care*, her dystopian novel, all the more so since Frame's own feelings of 'nothingness' experienced in hospital readily enabled her to identify with their suffering. Her literary models are European and British for the most part: the Brontës, Shelley, Keats, George Eliot, Thomas Hardy, to name but a few. And her seven-year exile (the object of the third volume of the Autobiography), one that is meant as a therapeutic escape for fear her country might again send her to a psychiatric hospital ('– I was a certified lunatic in New Zealand', *TAS* 20) is also the quest of the Pakehas, for the literary roots she needs in order to find 'a writing of her own'. At the end of the trilogy, when she returns to her country, she plans to be a 'mapmaker for those who will follow' (III 166), a literary pioneer, charting the way ahead.

The question of Frame being a woman writer is interesting when we consider the topics she deals with in her work. Feminist critic Luce Irigaray considers that women write much more, or much more openly, about their bodies than men do. We can readily assent to this since in Frame's Autobiography as well as in *Faces in the Water*, the body is central to the point of obsession, as it preys on her mind. To parody Judith Butler's title,[5] her body matters, also because women are far more under social pressure in body matters than men are. Frame's 'difference' is not merely mental. The numerous mentions of her red bushy hair, of her inadequate clothes, of her ungraceful shape, are revealing enough of her preoccupations. In *Faces in the Water*, the body is seen at its most repulsive: the smells, the oozing liquids, the 'animalization' of the patients. The obsession with death, illness, exclusion and isolation is the raw material of a writing that is not, however, devoid of humour. Even the story of a life that is more akin to a tragedy is relieved by humorous passages that are absent from the pages of *Faces in the Water* and *Owls Do Cry*, as if it had been easier to tell the truth under the guise of fiction, and no doubt it was.

I will start by analysing Frame's two autobiographical novels, *Owls Do Cry* and *Faces in the Water*. Then I shall consider her fictional works – the nine novels, the short stories and the poems – before finally analysing the 'official' Autobiography. Only one novel – *The Carpathians* – was published after it during her lifetime and the novella, *Towards Another Summer*, written in 1963, was published posthumously. I want to demonstrate that the Autobiography can be taken as an analeptic or hermeneutic tool – a precious key – with which to reread the novels, given that it sheds a retrospective light on her works, all of which belong to this autobiographical space. I also mean to show that most of the fiction is, so to speak, framed in by autobiography. In Frame's case, it is as if the self could not be contained in the restrictive space of an autobiography but was disseminated throughout all the works. Be it in fiction or autobiography, Frame's favoured narrators are often children or people who are 'different' (even mad), 'they' as she calls them, those who live 'on the rim of the farthest circle' whether it is a geographical, mental or social rim (and she has had a taste of all three). My decision to deal with the Autobiography last is explained and justified by the importance this work occupies in the whole of her production. It is indeed thanks to the Autobiography and to Jane Campion's film that Frame won international fame, even though she was already famous among intellectual and literary circles. The book seems to depend on the film: most people, myself included, saw the film first and then wanted to read the book. So in our perception, the book exists 'retroactively' and the same could apply to her fiction and poetry. In his article on Foucault and Frame, Jean-Jacques Lecercle says (perhaps somewhat exaggeratedly) that Frame's novels, poetry and even short stories might have been forgotten but for the Autobiography. To some extent, I share this analysis, at least from a French perspective. I also think that the Autobiography is a greater literary achievement than any of her other works, although this is not a view shared by most other critics. It is, however, thanks to this Autobiography that Frame herself has become a myth, the New Zealand writer *par excellence*, whose uncommon life might of course account for the readers' interest, even fascination. It is true that such a life may explain the success of the book (had her life been more ordinary, her Autobiography would probably have been less successful). It is as if the readers – and this is what Frame deplores – were more interested in her life than in her writing (also the case for the Brontës in their time), which may be true, though her talent as a writer has turned this life into a literary object that leads 'a life of its own'. The story of her life has become the life of this story,[6] a story that has become a myth.

2

The Autobiographical Novels

OWLS DO CRY: AUTOBIOGRAPHICAL NOVEL OR FICTIONAL AUTOBIOGRAPHY?

Owls Do Cry is Frame's first novel, published in 1958. She evidently borrowed some material for it from her own life, for, as she said: 'reality, the ore of polished the fiction' (III 19). Yet she also makes it clear that the book is a novel, despite the resemblances between Daphne and herself, Toby and her brother Robert and Chicks and her younger sister June. The title is inspired by *The Tempest*, and that sets the tone for the whole book. Like Ariel, the fairy spirit who shifts between two worlds, most of the characters in the novel are somewhat otherworldy.

Written in the third person singular, except for Chick's diary (a sort of embedded autobiography), it opens with Daphne's narrative, related to us from the psychiatric hospital – 'the dead room' – to which she has been confined. Daphne's family name, Withers, significantly underlines the limits and eventual atrophy imposed by a conformist society: 'The Withers have atrophied in their stereotypes'. Gina Mercer thinks the family name is borrowed from Greville Texidor's story 'Anyone Home?' (*SF* 33) where the family name is also Withers. It is, however, no wonder that Frame's fiction should be peopled with characters whose difference is punished, even annihilated.

That is precisely what happens to Milly Galbraith in *Intensive Care*, Frame's frightful dystopia that borrows its binary system of classification between animals and humans from George Orwell's *Brave New World*. Difference is articulated in language. Daphne's is poetic, even prophetic, though it is considered as 'the language of the mad' by 'normal' people. The difference is rendered typographically through the use of italics. All the characters who stand against the tyranny of social conformism share a common abnegation from the established codes of communication either because they are below or beyond words.

The very title of the novel *The Edge of the Alphabet* is significant: those who are different, who do not conform, speak 'beyond the alphabet', 'beyond the range of words' (*EA* 16), 'beyond the boundaries of words' (*EA* 18). Frame's originality lies in her questioning language, reproaching it with being one of the main causes of the individual's alienation in society, though she is aware that it is a 'necessary evil' for how is one to say that language is alienating without simultaneously using it to do so? Language is very ambivalent 'a mixture of jewels and waste' (*Ca* 127). It is both an object of fascination, the key to dreams and imagination but also an object of fear and distrust since it can both betray and destroy, as she reapeatedly shows in various episodes in the Autobiography, ranging from the comic to the tragic. Language can be the vector of false values and eventually an obstacle to communication between people: 'But it is imperative, for our own survival, that we avoid one another, and what more successful means of avoidance are there than words? Language will keep us safe from human onslaught, will express for us our regret at being unable to supply groceries of love or peace'. (*EA* 55) This highly critical vision of a stereotyped language as an obstacle to communication is one of Frame's leitmotifs.

The book opens with an italicized one-page prologue told by Daphne from the hospital, called the dead room, the very name Frame also uses in *Faces in the Water*. But 'We do not know who Daphne is, and won't know for certain until we have deciphered the representation of electric shock treatment in chapter thirteen'.[1] Oettli-van Delden insists on the deliberate confusion created by the narrator whose voice sometimes overlaps with Daphne's, 'thereby implying her solidarity with the latter's perspective'.[2]

This incipit is like a replica of *The Catcher in the Rye* written in 1951 by J. D. Salinger, where Holden is also in a psychiatric ward from which he tells his story in the first person singular. That makes it sound more autobiographical of course, though, as Philippe Lejeune reminds us, autobiography is not reduced to the use of the first person pronoun. The 'I' could just be grammatical, without any further equation beween the speaking subject and the living author. In fact, *Owls Do Cry* is probably more autobiographical than *The Catcher in the Rye* where the use of the first person may be as much of a literary trick as the use of the third can be to hide one's own real story. In *Living in the Maniototo*, the narrator speaks about 'the enormous burden upon the "I" to tell all, while viewing through the narrow I-shaped window that restricted the vision and allowed only occasional arrows to be fired with no guarnatee that they would pierce the armour of "otherness" worn by the characters of the book' (*LM* 61). Writing an autobiography may well impose upon the I 'the enormous burden to tell all'. For example, it is easier for the author to relate her experiences in psychiatric hospitals in her fiction than in the Autobiography, because being fictional, it is easier for 'normal people' to bear than their proximity to the 'mad' subject, without being frightened. It might also be a way for the writer to invite her readers to read all her works, moving from one to the other and finding in one what is lacking in the other. That is so even though, once we have read the Autobiography, we can be sure that Frame borrowed a lot from her real life to write both *Owls Do Cry* and *Faces in the Water*. Francie is but a replica of Myrtle, Frame's eldest sister who drowned in the local swimming pool. Making her fictional Myrtle die in the flames is a way of hiding the real event, though she actually inserts some 'true' autobiographical elements in the episode of Francie's death: the doctor's visit to announce her death is reproduced in the Autobiography almost verbatim.

I will articulate my analysis of the book around the three main characters who respectively embody three modes of living, speaking three different kinds of language: Daphne's is poetic or prophetic, Chicks' is fraught with clichés, whereas Toby stands in an uncomfortable in-betweenness, as emblematic of a third voice or way (the French *voix* and *voie* are interesting homophones). The division of the book into two parts – past and present – is also revealing of the gap between the world of children, and that of adults. Daphne refuses to grow up, whereas Chicks desperately clings to what she thinks is the perfect image of adulthood; Toby is caught between those two extremes, unable to give up the world of childhood, albeit unable to fit in the world of adults either.

'Talk of treasure' is the title of the first part of the novel. The treasure is none other than the rubbish dump (the 'controlling trope'[3] of the novel) where the children repeatedly go to find the bits and pieces that society has rejected (as it does everything old, different or useless). These include a copy of Grimm's *Fairy-Tales*, which Janet says she had discovered and loved in the first volume of the Autobiography. Gina Mercer among others sees the rubbish dump as the female space par excellence: 'Initially, the four form a community, enclosed by the sheltering female 'hollow' of the rubbish dump. To them that hollow is warm, nurturing, a source of treasure and creative fulfillment. To conventional culture, as represented by Bob and Amy Withers, it is dirty, dangerous, a source of disease and decay, with only destructive potential.' (*SF* 33) I would argue rather that the rubbish dump is a kind of prelapsarian world, a paradise (soon to be lost) where the children – and this is probably highly significant – are together. Never is this sense of community so strongly established as in childhood, before the death of Francie, the eldest. What dominates in this first part of the narration is the use of the pronouns 'they' and 'we', as opposed to the individualized 'I's of the second section. This does not mean that all identities are subsumed into a coherent whole: differences between the children are made visible from the start. Whereas Daphne sees treasures in the ledgers they find, Toby sees mere 'sums, grown-up sums' (*ODC* 15) in anticipation of his later obsession with money. Beauty is for those who can see it, and adults are blind to it. Francie declares: 'grown-ups are silly' (*ODC* 36) before (literally) falling into 'their' world at the cost of her life. Toby's other obsession, as a means to protect and reassure himself, is with maps: 'A map is the supreme trope of power and control'.[4] The rubbish dump is a ground for exploration, and adventure (a fetish word for the child Janet), even if the adventure might prove dangerous, even fatal, as Francie's death testifies.

The reader is told about her death in a prolepsis, before it actually takes place some thirty pages later, as if she dies twice, once as the Joan of Arc she impersonated at school before doing it 'for good' on the rubbish dump: 'On the last day of school Francie is dressed as Joan of Arc in the school play, 'in a silver helmet and breastplate waiting to be burned', and enacts the sacrifice that she is to make in reality later at the dump, the sacrifice necessitated by the search for treasure'.[5] Francie's death is an illustration of the mixture of fact and fiction that Frame so often and playfully resorts to:

> Well, I am always in fictional mode, and autobiography is found fiction. I look at everything from the point of view of fiction, and so it wasn't a change to be writing autobiography except the autobiography was more restrictive because it was based in fact, and I wanted to make an honest record of my life. But I was still bound by the choice of words and the shaping of the book, and that is similar to when one is writing fiction. I think that in writing there's no feeling of returning to or leaving a definite form, it's all in the same country, and within view of one's imaginative home so to speak, or in the same town. They are different and each has its own interests.[6]

She conflates the real event of her elder sister's drowning (a key episode in the Autobiography) and Francie's fictional death in the flames, as the announcement of her death by the doctor – reproduced verbatim in the Autobiography – testifies. 'Frame collapses the tragedies of Myrtle and Isabel into one, thereby intensifying the experience of death',[7] which is close to the pain felt during the ECT sessions, where the two kinds of death are evoked: 'They fear drowning. Or burning' (*ODC* 46). In both fact and fiction, the sister's death is a turning point in Janet/ Daphne's life as it seems to be a fall into adulthood, a passage from innocence to experience (which reinforces my analysis of the rubbish dump as a prelapsarian world). This is how Francie explained it to Daphne:

> When you're grown up, you're frightened to taste the nice things, like Easter eggs, in case you never get them again, or something, so you save them up till you have rooms full of them. It's like spending money and being afraid because you've spent it; only this isn't money, it's something inside people that they're afraid to spend. I know, from Mawhinney's and other places. And then you die, and leave yourself and the nice things wrapped up, like an Easter egg, with the lovely wavery paper still on it, and the black patterned chocolate inside. (*ODC* 36)

This passage is an obvious echo to the beginning of volume II in the Autobiography, when Janet and her youngest sister discover their aunt's untasted chocolates, and (as children) cannot resist 'testing them'. At this point in the narration, and in the children's lives, Francie has already taken her distance from her younger siblings, refusing their childish games, to play more serious ones with Tim (her younger sister's future husband).

Her fall into this sacrificial fire seems to trigger the tragic destiny of all the members of the Withers family. It also gives Daphne a more definite role, replacing the eldest she has now become after her sister's death. W. D. Ashcroft sees Francie as being transmogrified into Daphne, since her death 'precipitates Daphne's plunge through the borders of sanity'[8] with Daphne ironically ending up in the very same work place as Francie. Things will have turned full circle: there is no way out from a stifling society. Daphne's hallucinations (or should we call them magic, fairy-tale like visions?) start just after the accident, when her perceptions of time, space and objects are distorted into a kind of parody of *Alice in Wonderland*: 'so she put the cake in a dish, beside a packet of needles and a wad of darning wool, and the seedcake sprouted into a tall gold flower growing up through the roof and further than the sky, and Daphne saw it, and picked one of its petals to take home in the car' (*ODC* 41).

Nature is omnipresent in the novel, though often as threatening presence, culminating in the description Daphne makes of nurse Flora Norris and 'her face cut through with the wire from the dream nasturtium' (*ODC* 133). Daphne's mental confusion (or difference?) is rendered in the narrative structure as well, when the first episode of the ECT session (that should belong to part II) interrupts the narration of part I, as if the narrator meant to prepare the reader for the horror of the psychiatric hospital, the place that has become her second home. The descriptions of the life in hospital may not be as realistically drawn as in *Faces in the Water* (which Frame baptizes 'documentary fiction'); they are, however, more numerous and detailed (even though in poetic form) than in the far more elliptical Autobiography. The world of the hospital is dominated by the omnipotent figure of the doctor, 'God or the devil' (*ODC* 46) who rules over a herd of women nurses and patients (the difference is sometimes almost obliterated), who are reified and silenced while the ECT machine becomes a mistress under the doctor's touch: 'He stands with his hand resting lightly, it seems lightly, upon his treasure; then Daphne knows he dare not move his hand away from the voluptuous body of the red and black-eyed machine, which, in case of escape, is fastened, as a lover secures the object of his love with cords of habit' (*ODC* 47). 'The Doctor is slavishly and pathologically in love with his EST machine',[9] neglecting to talk to his patients; the latters' voices are never to be heard, because in the eyes of the staff, they are not even human. The main activities of these patients are, as Gina Mercer convincingly argues, traditionally female ones, such as knitting or sewing (an echo to the short story 'The Bedjacket' but also to the character of Milly in *Intensive Care*, whose sewing, she hopes, will save her), which are encouraged by the staff as possible means of communication: 'How would Daphne like to make something, a scarf, or basket, wouldn't Daphne like to make something, and go up to the class in the park with the other people; and knit and weave and sew, and not be here alone all day with no one to talk to?' (*ODC* 151).

According to Frame, people often address children or 'mad' people in the third person singular, as if they were unable to understand or answer for themselves, to which the repetition of the interrogation also testifies. '"They", "she"...I mean children are forever "they" until they grow up,[10] the Benvenistian "non-person"'.[11]

The routine of the hospital is sometimes interrupted by events, such as balls (*Faces in the Water* also stages two of them where the female patients are made-up like stage dolls, or like Ciss Everest in *Intensive Care*), which are a sad parody of 'real life' ones. In hospital, everything consists in 'doing as if', in pretending the patients are 'real/normal people'. In reality, however, the staff do everything they can to convince them they are not: 'all dressed up *as if* they were real people' (*ODC* 144; italics mine). The patients cannot win: either they behave like the mad people they are supposed to be, thus confirming the diagnosis of madness, or they try (or are forced to) behave more 'normally', in which case they are equally regarded as mad, because they are parodying the normality they are (supposedly) deprived of. Daphne's reaction on hearing about her mother's death is a perfect example of the inability of the staff to understand her. Her dancing the foxtrot goes against what is expected in such circumstances: she transgresses all the rules of decency, which precipitates the decision to have her lobotomized, as if the staff had only waited for this blatant proof of her madness. Her mind needs fixing for her to fit in, 'cut and tailored to the ways of the world' (*FW* 217). Just before the operation, Daphne's father and brother come to visit her, terrified of the place that looks more like a gothic fortress or a prison than a hospital. Fearing being sucked into her world of madness if he stays too long in hospital, Toby has an epileptic fit that prevents him from seeing his sister, whom the puzzled father meets alone. A strange dialogue takes place between father and daughter where Daphne asks him to name all the members of the family, even though she seems to have failed to recognize him. The lobotomy appears as the panacea; Teresa/Chicks believes in its efficiency, though the father has doubts.

The epilogue of the novel has been criticized as an awkward attempt, on Frame's part, to present a devastating picture of an over-conformist society going mad: 'The epilogue is a heavy-handed attempt to make the Withers world a universal world and to hammer home the main theme of the book'.[12] Ironically enough, the only worthy survivor is Daphne who, after her operation, has been promoted assistant forewoman, an echo to the Autobiography (and to *Faces in the Water*) where normality is equated with making hats. 'Frame could be saying: (a) the world is so crazy that one can only cope if one's brain is amputated; (b) the so-called 'mad' person with only half a brain functions better than the so-called 'sane'; (c) those who have imagination are dealt with by means of brain surgery'.[13] But she certainly never suggests that lobotomy should be the remedy. Like Nola in the Autobiography (whose luck it was not to win a prize, and who might be a fictional version of Janet Frame's friend Audrey Scrivener), Daphne undergoes the lobotomy that Frame and her other fictional double, Istina Mavet, are fortunately spared. The lobotomy is supposed to 'darn the believed crevice of my world' (*ODC* 170). Gina Mercer notices the number of images of holes, cavities, pockets, in which creativity could blossom but which society is too frightened to allow them to blossom.

By the end, Toby has become the tramp he had seen in his dream of the three witches (another Shakespearean echo?) and the father is still barely alive, a picture of desolation and solitude. As for Teresa, she is shot in the head by her husband, not unlike Bessick's wife, whom she can at last resemble!

Chicks/Teresa is an anti-Daphne, who confuses having and

being. It is significant that she should never be given direct access to the narration. It is only through her thirty-page diary that she is given a voice, as if it were controlled/framed in by Daphne's more authentic voice. Teresa is a sort of onomastic palimpsest for Chicks (that sounds less chic), playing the same role as make-up, covering an undesired identity: 'She adopts an entirely false voice and pays much attention to her make-up, just as a child will *make-up* stories, both constructing an artificial reality' (*SF* 36; JF's italics). Her stereotyped superficial language is fraught with clichés, the linguistic expression of her desperate wish to conform, to do the right things, wear the right clothes, read the right books, entertain the right people, with the hope of suppressing any trace of difference that could alienate her from the rest of 'the world that matters', to the point of renouncing part of her self, to the extent that she is hardly a convincing character. If she could, she would make a tabula rasa of her embarrassing family (an epileptic brother and a mad sister) and of the past. Difference is perceived as a severe handicap in a society that severely condemns it. 'The idea still prevailed that mental illness was a form of childish naughtiness which might be cured in a Victorian environment with the persuasion of stern speech and edifying literature' (*FW* 238).

Frame uses scathing irony to denounce this creed, through a ferocious portrait of her fictional youngest sister. The main part of her diary is concerned with the preparations for the visit of Dr Bessick and his wife. That constitutes a key event in her life. She wishes she could speak French with them as a sign of education. She wants to discuss the right kind of music and literature (like Beatrice in *The Rainbirds*, she reads the Brontës, who are among Frame's favourites, as the poem 'Haworth Parsonage, Mt Maunganui' (*PM* 34) testifies). It is of course extremely ironical that Be/sick should kill his wife not long after this visit, thus destroying his perfect image in the eyes of an incredulous Teresa. This murder paves the way to the over-pessimistic ending of the novel, where she is herself killed by her own husband, in an ironical replica of this first murder. It is only when she hears the news of her mother's death that Teresa becomes Chicks again for a very short while. The change is rendered typographically with the use of the italics, these being usually Daphne's prerogative. It is as if her fears of becoming

Daphne-like were becoming fulfilled. But she pulls herself together with the revealing declaration: 'Back to *normal*' (*ODC* 119; italics mine). Her plan to return to her native town and have a house built on the old site of the rubbish dump might tally with her wish to erase the past, in a gesture similar to her adoption of a new identity: 'it's filled in and you shan't see it' (*ODC,* 127). Her death at the end might be read as the failure of her shallow materialistic dreams.

Society and its values have killed them. Chicks will always remember that she was not properly dressed to go to a ball and was thus never invited for a dance. And Amy, the mother, remembers her spying on wealthy people 'on the other side' of the window. They will always remain 'on the other side'. After reading Chicks' diary, Toby thrusts it into the fire and leaves a house where he is not welcome. Toby's difference, like Bruddie's in the Autobiography, is his epilepsy. And despite the mother's comforting creed that illness might be the sign of genius, he never fits in a society which has labelled him different. Toby, like Daphne, is an outsider, regarded as other because of his epilepsy and poverty. He sees the options chosen by Chicks and Daphne, but cannot wholly adopt either of their polarised positions. Like his homonym in *The Edge of the Alphabet*, he is in-between. 'He is far enough outside of the norm to be critical of it, at times expressing himself in a seer-like and lyrical voice, similar to Daphne's [...]. At other times though, Toby denies this kind of knowledge and strives to find satisfaction in materialism.' (*SF,* 37) He, too, has fallen into the world of adults, though he is never fully integrated into it. He is neither an adult nor a child, neither a 'real' man, nor a woman, but an exceptionally mediocre character, the anti-hero: 'the man who is given the vocation of failure'.[13] Fay Chalkin (a milder version of Teresa) marries someone else, ironically sending him a piece of her wedding cake, as if all he could get were bits and pieces of a happy life that is not meant for him. His dream of the three sisters/witches that follows the gift of the cake verges on the nightmare ending in his premonitory homelessness: 'There is no place for me' (*ODC* 80). Toby is one of 'the lonely people':[15] 'Toby Withers, the shingle-short with the dirty fingernails and the brown greasy hair and the heavy shoulders and the head on one side and the thick neck with valleys of flesh at the hairline' (*ODC* 62). 'Toby is reduced to a sum of negative features, objectified by the repetition of the definite article'.[16] As Alice Braun convincingly argues, he is rejected not so much by society at large (like Daphne) as by the microcosmic community of Waimaru. His end seems to actualize the dream in which he didn't know where to go: 'Epileptic convicted for being a vagabond and lacking visible means of support' (*ODC* 172). 'From a label there is no escape'.[17] Toby is forever branded by his shameful illness: there is no place for him anywhere.

The reader never, however, has the feeling that Daphne is happy. Simone Oettli-van Delden insists that Frame's view is a bit schematic and rather intolerant; it is as though the only option for her is between two extremes. You are either over-materialistic, hence ridiculous, like Chicks. Or, on the other hand, you are poetic, imaginative and artistic, but unable to express this creativity because it goes against the values of a society that rejects you for being what you are to the point of putting you in a mental home and even lobotomizing you in order to make you 'conform'. In a word, you cannot win.

> Few readers would deny the validity of Frame's attack on the materialism and the abuse of language, power and technology that characterize Western society, and they are likely to sympathize with her powerful and convincing evocation of the inner world of those who are its victims. But she undermines her own persuasiveness by the unrelenting aridity of her perspective on the adult world, by her determination to generalize the negative aspects of society to such an extent that they are made to represent the whole, and by her claim that a true awareness of the negative aspects of society is the exclusive prerogative of either children, the handicapped, or the mad, who are thus granted exceptional but ultimately self-destructive insight. The process of reaching adulthood involves confronting these aspects in a more constructive way than any of the Withers children can manage. Death, madness or marginality are not the only alternatives to an espousal of hypocritical, materialistic and oppressive social norms, yet this is the message the 'language of the mad' is often made to convey in Frame's novels.[18]

It is true that Frame doesn't seem to leave many options: her choice is clear but frightening. The reader cannot be but tempted to follow the path of poetry and imagination, but the cost is high. It is as if there was no possible cohabitation between imagination and society, as if the two worlds could not coexist, which seems to invalidate what Frame says in the Autobiography: 'I wanted an imagination that would inhabit a world of fact' (I 126). But to moderate Oettli's harsh judgement of the book, I would suggest that *Owls Do Cry* may be excessive in order to prove more efficacious. The humour of the Autobiography is absent here, which might be due to Frame's age at the time of her writing this first novel. With the Autobiography (written at around 60) she had already taken a safe, critical, humorous distance, as if to illustrate what a critic says: 'complaining is the death of art, smiling its salvation'.[19]

FACES IN THE WATER

'I was put in hospital because a great gap opened in the ice floe between myself and the other people whom I watched' (*FW* 10).

Frame herself calls *Faces in the Water* 'a documentary fiction', a sort of oxymoric title as the qualifier hints at a realistic account, whereas 'fiction' denies it. That is, however, in keeping with Frame's habit of manipulating her reader, or of equating fact and fiction. 'The book therefore evades generic classification in that it incorporates elements from three different genres: the documentary, the novel and autobiography'.[20] In volume III of the Autobiography, Frame gives an account of the genesis of the book. It was written to follow the London psychiatrist's advice: 'It was his opinion also that as I was obviously suffering from the effects of my stay in hospital in New Zealand, I should write my story of that time to give me a clearer view of my future' (III 128). The aim of the book was initially therapeutic:

> I began to write the story of my experiences in hospitals in New Zealand, recording faithfully every happening and the patients and the staff I had known, but borrowing from what I had observed among the patients to build a more credibly 'mad' central character, Istina Mavet, the narrator. Also planning a subdued rather than a sensational record, I omitted much, aiming more for credibility than a challenge to me by those who might disbelieve my record. (III 132-3)

The result, however, was a literary success, though she later regretted not having 'told all the truth': 'and were I to rewrite *Faces in the Water* I would include much that I omitted because I didn't want a record by a former patient to appear overdramatic' (II 99). The name Istina Mavet means *Truth* and *Death* – 'the Serbo-Croat word for truth with the Hebrew word for death' (*WA* 207) – but it might also phonetically refer to Frame herself: 'I Am'. The use of the first person was actually problematic as it was assumed Istina was Frame herself, which she emphatically denied in an interview: '*Faces in the Water* was autobiographical in the sense that everything happened but the central character was invented'.[21] As in the character of Francie in *Owls Do Cry*, she conflates some of the mad patients and herself in this portrait.

The three sections of the book correspond to the three (or rather two, since she comes back to Cliffhaven at the end) different hospitals where Istina Mavet undergoes a sort of descent into Hell. As in the Victorian period, mental illness is equated with sin or dangerous subversion, especially in women who threaten the patriarchal order embodied by the psychiatric hospital and its male doctors. *Faces in the Water* is not, however, an explicit autobiography. The use of the first person was misleading to the point that some critics had mistaken the heroine for Janet Frame herself. *Faces in the Water* is, however, 'a subdued record' where the narrator resorts to (black) humour to hide the almost unbearable experience of the hospital, which would otherwise be scary for 'normal' people.

As a world apart, physically relegated to the margins of society (like Manuka Home in *The Carpathians*), the hospital is structured hierarchically like the prison Istina constantly compares it with. The patients are put in hospital for the 'crime of difference' (a hint to Michel Foucault's *Surveiller et Punir*)[22] and it is difficult to see any attempt at curing the patients, who are submitted to harsh physical and mental tortures. Illness, be it physical or mental, is indeed perceived as a sin in a society that extols the values of conformity, obedience, adaptability. Inside, the hospital is ruled by omnipotent doctors (the gods of *Owls Do Cry*), who are at the top of the pyramid, with the nurses as replacements or inferior accomplices, transmitting orders, enforcing discipline, punishing. The only links with the external world are the rare visitors who, Istina thinks, may have a 'secret affinity' with the patients (*FW* 163), as if madness were infectious. And at the very bottom of this chain are the patients who, as in *Owls Do Cry*, are not even considered as human beings; Istina, as narrator, observer, guide, but also as one of 'them' takes pains to individualize them in a sometimes amusing gallery of portraits. The world of the hospital resembles a dystopian Brave New World, with its frightful classification. The patients could be its brainless epsilons.

THE HOSPITAL: A WORLD APART

Istina is sent to the two hospitals of Cliffhaven and Treecroft (which could be fictionalizations of Seacliff). Their names 'suggest their enclosing, imprisoning nature. A 'haven' is an enclosed piece of water, a harbour or port, or, more figuratively, a refuge. Likewise, a 'croft' is an enclosed piece of land' (SF 44-5). Though I partly agree with this analysis, I would rather insist on the ambivalent nature of the names, especially Cliffhaven (the danger of the cliff being compensated by the haven) which Mercer also underlines: the hospital might be a trap, but it is also a refuge, as Frame puts it in the Autobiography, which makes it all the more difficult to leave.

The two hospitals are pictured as isolated buildings, and difficult to reach: 'an aunt decided to "adopt" me and visit me each week, making a *long journey* by tram from the outskirts of the city' (FW 73; italics mine). Like its equivalent in *Owls Do Cry*, the hospital is more like a gothic fortress than the medical institution it is supposed to be:

> But I felt increasingly like a guest who is given every hospitality in a country mansion yet who finds in unexpected moments a trace of a mysterious presence; sliding panels; secret tappings; and at last surprises the host and hostess in clandestine conversations and plottings with mention of poison, torture, death. Or was I inhabiting, as it were, as guest for the week end, my own mind, and becoming more and more perturbed by its manifestations of evil? (FW 75)

It is as if unimaginable things, which must be kept secret, were taking place behind the high walls of a prison. The multiplicity of wards, that also follow a hierarchy (from best to worst) are like so many miniature prisons within the larger architecture of incarceration. The vocabulary used for patients could as well have been used for prisoners. The women are 'on parole', or 'on probation'. The narrator goes even further in her comparisons: the hospital is more like a concentration camp, and the staff so many Nazi soldiers: 'We stood there naked, packed tightly like cattle at the salesyards' (*FW* 94). The women are no better than beasts. Treating them as such turns them, through a kind of vicious performative circle, into the animals the staff believes them to be. Istina has entered another country as it were, a *terra incognita*, a strange land that will never really become familiar as adaptation might again confirm the diagnosis of madness, even if 'settling in' is the (ironical) *sine qua non* condition to liberation, 'to be able to live "out in the world"' (*FW* 42). But the longer one stays in hospital, the less the hope of escape; once in, always in. 'I was now an established citizen with little hope of returning across the frontier; I was in the crazy world, separated now by more than locked doors and barred windows from the people who called themselves sane' (*FW* 105). If Istina refuses (not always successfully) to adopt (or adapt to) the hospital, it seems to have absorbed her, in spite of her resistance. It is this resistance the staff means to crush, with the use of ECT and the more radical lobotomies the most rebellious patients are threatened with, and even some undergo. In its more metaphorical dimension, the hospital is a real hell which Marianne Camus analyzes in her article,[23] where one descends through a cascade of diminishing concentric circles, in a frightful spiral from which it is difficult even to climb back. In a word, the hospital fails to perform its etymological promises: it is anything but hospitable.

TWO 'SEPARATELY SEALED WORLDS' (*FW* 195)

What strikes the reader is the lack of communication between the staff and the patients, as if the former protected themselves behind the authority of their scientific (incomprehensible) language, which gives them the aura of semi-gods (*FW* 190–234): 'listening to the conversations of the Gods' (*FW* 234). Language is their instrument of domination: 'Istina is not to be taken in by this scientific knowledge, though she is aware it gives the doctors power over her and her life'.[24] The patriarchal order of the outside world is transposed inside the hospital, which appears like a microcosmic parody of the world at large.

As for the patients, though, Istina individualizes/catalogues the different doctors whose methods vary: 'There were doctors who 'got things done' and doctors who cut short whatever you were trying to say to them and doctors who spoke to you in a loud voice as if you couldn't hear properly and doctors who asked you strange questions' (*FW* 181). Dr Steward's method (like Dr Clapper's in *Scented Gardens for the Blind*) is based on seduction or propitiation, as he creates a (fake) intimacy with the patients as if they were his confidantes: 'My wife feels the same way [...] the technique at least was successful' (*FW* 180). There again, Istina sees through the doctor's strategy which is certainly more efficacious than harsh treatments and no dialogue, but just as dangerous. Noeline, one of the patients, develops what Alice Braun diagnoses as the 'Archambault syndrome' 'which is characterized by the delirious love one feels for another who is in a superiour social position'[25] (here a male doctor):

> And Poor Noeline, who was waiting for Dr Howell to propose to her although the only words he had ever spoken to her were How are you? Do you know where you are? Do you know why you are here? – phrases which ordinarily would be hard to interpret as evidence of affection [...]. So that when Dr Howell finally married the occupational therapist, Noeline was taken to the disturbed ward. (*FW* 30)

Istina's irony (a token of her difference) almost exonerates the doctor, whose only fault is to be young and handsome and who, unlike the majority of the staff, joins in the games with the patients, but she also explains and excuses Noeline, whose frustrations are shared by most of the patients and who invests emotionally in any (im)possible object of love. It is Dr Trace who first entrusts Istina with the care of serving tea to 'the Gods' as she ironically calls them, a first step on the way to normalization and civilization. His goodness leads her to have hallucinations of her grandfather: 'He was my grandfather and no doubt his pockets were full of striped mint lollies' (*FW* 233).

But the crucial decision not to lobotomize Istina is Dr Portman's whose advice Istina dares to ask in front of an incredulous Matron Glass: '"What is your opinion?" [...] "I say no", he said. "I don't want you changed. I want you to stay as you are"' (*FW* 218–19). Istina's 'house of self' – 'the central storehouse – that self was to be assaulted, perhaps demolished'

(*FW* 219) – will not be destroyed, the decision being equivalent to the word of God. The imagery of the self as a place/a house tallies with Mercer's analysis of the hospital as a territory with the patients in the role of colonized/uncivilized people to be conquered: 'she depicts the hospitals as isolated punitive colonies' (*SF* 46). Though it would be difficult to deny the validity of this analysis, Mercer seems to forget that the women patients were not the rightful occupants of the hospital territory, the latter never having been envisaged as an inhabitable place.[26]

If the doctors are seen as divine figures by the female patients, it is not so with the nurses, who relay their orders in much less subtle ways. But 'in spite of the influence of Matron Glass and Sister Bridge it was the doctor's decision which mattered' (*FW* 190). Unlike the doctors, they are nearer the patients whom they see everyday. Matron Glass is the caricature of the head nurse, who is sometimes reduced to her title alone: 'Matron'. '"What you need", Matron said to me, "is bringing to your senses. What you need is a stay in Ward Two"' (*FW* 135). She is the representative and executive of an authority embodied by the superior doctors. They believe in discipline to 'correct' madness. It is also through language that they rule, promising punishments 'for their own good'. As we will see in the third part, the prevalent feeling in the hospital is fear. There is the fear of ECT, but also, the vague, diffuse fear of any possible danger, which might be even worse for not being named: 'I was frightened of Matron Glass and her heavy sarcasm, her taunts, when I panicked or ran away, about "misbehavior" and "self-discipline" and her remarks that I ought to be used to life in hospital for I had been there long enough' (*FW* 134).

The role and function of the nurses is to maintain permanent control (or to make the patients believe that is what they do) over their inmates in an illustration of what Jeremy Bentham and Michel Foucault after him call 'panopticism',[27] thus inducing a permament feeling of guilt and the need to confess to an absent (hence less threatening) reader. In the following quotations, Matron and Sister Bridge could be just as frightening as God who, for some believers, can see and know everything and every sin one may have committed: 'It occurred to me, frighteningly, that Matron and Sister Bridge had known me all my life and had spied on me even when I was a child. They must have seen me steal money, and pinch the baby on its arm, and sneak the doctor's book from the top of the wardrobe' (*FW* 153). As for Sister Bridge (whose name might signify a possible link with the patients), she seems to be a favourite with them. Despite a rather disgraceful physical appearance – Istina compares her to a female butcher (*FW* 139) – 'her attitude was usually one of happy sarcasm' (*FW* 139). But reversing the traditional roles, Istina 'observed Sister Bridge too closely' (*FW* 140), which the latter resents. So she makes her pay for it, 'seizing every opportunity to hurt me' (*FW* 140). When Istina runs away and is caught up by Sister Bridge, the latter first resorts to the seductive method of the doctors to propitiate a reluctant Istina who hallucinates her into her mother (whom she both hates and loves), offering her an ice cream, showing her her house, before relapsing into her usual cruel sarcasms: 'Get into the dayroom, rag bag, and don't try anything with me' (*FW* 175). Which in turn provokes Istina's violence and despair: 'I pushed her in the back and she fell, with a cry of anger and pain' (*FW* 175), followed by the victim's renewed insults: 'You bitch. You cunning bitch!' (*FW* 176).

The only contact with the outside world comes from the rare visitors, whom the patients call 'The Ladies' (the very ironical title used for the patients by the nurses when they give them orders). The patients despise them, because they do not know how to behave: 'They were not sure how to talk to us or what to say; they had learned somewhere that a fixed smile was necessary, therefore they smiled' (*FW* 162), adopting the cliché attitude Istina (and Frame behind her) so severely condemns. And like the nurses, they see the patients as animals, Carol being a particularly interesting example: '"The Ladies" reacted to Carol as a zoologist might when meeting for the first time a species that conforms to all the generalizations made about it. Carol was the perfect "mental patient"' (*FW* 164), an echo to Janet's sarcasms about young psychologist John Forrest with whom she plays the perfect 'textbook schizophrenic' (**II 81**), as if it was necessary (or polite) to please the professionals (or the 'normal' people), to reward them for their efforts at trying, by 'playing the game', however dangerous this may prove, however ambivalent, too, as Janet/Istina also adopts the cliché attitudes she denounces in others.

'PERFORMING IS AS GOOD AS THE REAL THING'[28]

The other individualized visitor (as opposed to the group of Ladies) is Aunt Rose: 'Aunt Rose was my constant visitor [...] she seemed more to belong to other children; for you see I felt myself to be a child [...] wondering what she had brought me' (*FW* 104). The methods of the hospital infantilize the patients who, like children (and we might add like colonized people, as the Maori woman Hene tells Mattina in *The Carpathians*) 'are forever "they", unable to speak for themselves and reduced to obey the orders of the Gods or their substitutes. The bag Aunt Rose gives Istina becomes her only possession, 'to put my treasures in' (*FW* 105). As in *Living in the Maniototo*, where Mrs Tyndall, who is about to die, desperately clings to her carrier bag, as if it were her most precious possession or her only remaining link with the world. On his visit to his daughter, Istina's father tells her that her aunt is dead, depriving her of any further contact with the outside world.

It is only at the end that, having escaped the lobotomy, Istina is free to leave the hospital and write her story. 'The stories of this modern Scheherazade trying to escape the annihilation of the lobotomy will become *Faces in the Water* [...] and she becomes a poetess of madness'.[29] Unlike her unfortunate fellow-sufferers, Istina manages to climb back to give her frightening testimony.

> She provides an 'anatomy' of female mental 'disorders' in the 1950s: Maria, who has been in a European concentration camp (*FW* 107), and Josie, deserted by her American Marine husband (*FW* 230), are products (*and victims*) of a specific historical era (italics my addition). There are other problems which are less time and place specific. Frame catalogues: Maude, who [thinks she] is God; Dame Mary-Margaret, the controller of Egypt; Hilary who brings to 'her dedicated desperate search for the 'right man' a single-mindedness that would have been a credit to any scientist in his laboratory' (*FW* 178). [...] There is also Carol, the illegitimate dwarf, who has lived in the hospital since the age of twelve; [...] or Mrs Everett who, as an inexperienced, overwrought young mother, had murdered her little girl (*FW* 42). (*SF* 45)

This gallery of portraits is both tragic and comic, as if Istina meant (as Janet Frame does in the Autobiography) to entertain the reader who would otherwise be just as terrified as the visiting Ladies: 'Their faces would show just a hint of panic' (FW 164). 'The family talked jokingly of my having been in the 'nuthouse', and I gave them what they seemed to want – amusing descriptions of patients whose symptoms corresponded to the popular idea of the insane; and I described myself as if, by misfortune, I had been put among people, who, unlike myself, were truly ill' (FW 127). As in *Owls Do Cry*, the process of recivilization is based upon the enforcement of domestic (feminine) tasks, such as sewing, knitting or cleaning, at which Alice has become a champion. By accepting these menial tasks, which however gives them a certain (their only) dignity in the eyes of the staff, they might escape the dreaded ECT sessions. Istina shows that she distinguishes herself by her taste for books, which only Dr Portman perceives and encourages by letting her into the library van, to the dismay of the chaplain: 'No patient is allowed' (FW 241). Here again, Istina feels both like 'a patient [who] could not be trusted [and] the child [who] would not grasp the content' (FW 241). If inmates do not conform to the staff's expectations, do not behave as 'normal' patients, they are punished. If they do, it is the manifest proof of their madness. The process of civilization is hardly convincing or efficient. As Istina repeatedly shows, the patients (I would like to emphasize the etymology of the word which means 'suffering') are either reified or animalized. There is an insistence on bodies, smells, decay.

Mercer stresses Frame's audacity in having dared to write about such taboo subjects. What Frame avoids, says Mercer again, is the 'topics of avoidance themselves', such as death, illness and sex.[30] In *Faces in the Water*, madness is also a bodily matter, as if madness had a specific smell. Istina speaks of the 'ward body odor' (FW 71), as if the mad could not control their bodies. In the Autobiography, the father punishes Toby for his epileptic fits which he thinks he could put an end to if he wanted, because 'epilepsy is a sort of "bodily misbehaviour"'.[31] The orders of the staff are actually aimed at regulating the patients' disorders. The enterprise of re-education consists, ironically or paradoxically, in forcing them to urinate in public. This reinforces their 'animality' and justifies the staff's view that they are indeed animals: 'I would slide from my seat under the table and wet on the floor like an animal' (*FW* 95). Cleanliness is godliness; and dirt is vice. Frame refuses any romantic idealization of madness and through her narrator/guide, leads us into the real, terrifying, disgusting world of the mad. Even the attempts at normality are failures or sad parodies. As in *Owls Do Cry*, the ball is a pathetic gathering of clowns:

> Yes we danced, the crazy people from Ward Two whom even the people from the observation ward and the convalescent ward looked upon as oddities and loonies. We dressed in our exotic party dresses, taffetas and rayons and silk jersey florals, and we lined up outside the clinic to have make-up put on our faces from the ward box with its stump of lipstick, coated and roughened powder puffs, box of blossom-pink powder and scent bottle squirting carnation scent behind our ears [...] and in the hollow of our wrists. By the time we were ready we were a garden of carnations and we looked like stage whores. (*FW* 186)

This reads like a perfect illustration of Elaine Showalter's analysis of the 'lunatics' ball': 'For most observers, the fascination of the lunatics' ball was the illusion of normality it presented. Seen at such close range and in holiday settings, madness was no longer a gross and unmistakable inversion of appropriate conduct, but a collection of slightly disquieting gestures and postures.'[32]

In *Owls Do Cry*, the patients are told they must dance. Dancing is part of the re-education programme like the ECT sessions that punctuate and interrupt the daily routine. Mercer sees the ECT as the modern equivalent of the stake, or, I would suggest, of the electric chair. Both Istina and Daphne compare it to an assassination for the pain it gives: 'The fear of EST overlaps with another profound fear that runs throughout Frame's work, the fear of death'.[33] The patients wear woollen socks against the cold, hoping it might also ward off or diminish the pain. Though the staff insists on its therapeutic efficiency, from the point of view of the patients, it is a punishment for their unnamed crimes. No wonder that, like ill-treated children, the patients' main feeling should be a constant fear of doing wrong, of not behaving in the expected way, of being what they are. The climax of the process of re-education is the lobotomy Istina is threatened with to change her faulty personality. 'I will be 'retrained' – that is the word used for lobotomy cases.

Rehabilitated. Fitted, my mind cut and tailored to the ways of the world' (*FW* 217). As in the Autobiography, and to Janet/ Istina's dismay, the 'mother had signed the paper' (*FW* 215). Though she had sworn that no child of hers would ever spend time in Seacliff. 'But I was a child of hers, wasn't I? Wasn't I?' (II 74). It is 'the strange doctor' who decides to perform the operation because Istina has been 'naughty'. In *Wrestling With The Angel*, Michael King says that, even at the time, most doctors doubted the efficacy of a lobotomy: 'There was an eventual consensus that the harmful effects outweighed likely benefits' (*WA* 112).

On the announcement of the coming lobotomy, Istina, like Janet in the Autobiography, feels homeless with 'no place to stay' (*FW* 215), finding no refuge anywhere. Again, Istina resorts to the metaphor of the house to talk about her self: 'my personality had been condemned, like a slum dwelling' (*FW* 216), and she must be 'evicted' from this insalubrious site. But Istina, like Janet, but unlike Daphne or Nola (her friend 'who was not lucky enough to have won a prize') will not undergo the lobotomy, will not go and sell hats as one of the lobotomized now does in *Faces in the Water* or work at the mill like Daphne. Istina has other plans for her future. The end of the book is a climax of irony: "when you leave hospital you must forget all you have ever seen, put it out of your mind completely as if it never happened, and go and live a normal life in the outside world'. And by what I have written in this *document* you will see, won't you, that I have obeyed her?' (*FW* 254; italics mine).

3

'The House of Fiction'

In her study of Frame's novels, Karin Hansson draws the reader's attention to the importance of remembering 'that autobiographies are usually disguised novels, just as many novels are disguised autobiographies'.[1]

Most critics have convincingly divided Frame's fiction into two periods. I will more or less follow this chronological classification, too, though while respecting Frame's own refusal and defiance of any categorization, I want to insist on the obvious thematic, philosophical and narrative links between all the texts, bearing in mind my notion of the autobiographical prism none of them seems to escape. Also, for the sake of clarity and convenience, I will not strictly follow the chronology: for example, though *Towards Another Summer* was published posthumously, it had been written twenty years before the Autobiography. I include it in my last but one section, to emphasize the link with the Autobiography, as it bears obvious autobiographical features together with poetic passages. As for the novels, what interests me most is also their autobiographical tinge, whether it is explicit (in the choice of the characters' names for example), or more discrete (through some fleeting references to real events or situations). They are all concerned with Frame's favourite themes such as death, exclusion, illness, exile and literary creation, as if the novels were but the illustration of her strong belief in the power of imagination.

The first period involves *The Edge of the Alphabet*, *Scented Gardens for the Blind*, *The Adaptable Man*, *A State of Siege* and *Intensive Care*, and the second, the last three novels *Daughter*

Buffalo, *Living in the Maniototo* and *The Carpathians* where, as Mercer convincingly argues, optimism substitutes for the sheer pessimism of the first novels, and where the figure of the artist is perhaps more visible and more successful. It is as if Frame had at last found the Mirror City that she has always been looking for. The first novels could be encapsulated in the sentence I borrow from Janet Frame's first autobiographical volume: 'on the rim of the farthest circle' (I 117) and I will deal with the characters who are on the rim, on the edge, 'all the lonely people' such as Toby, Zoe, Malfred, Vera, who are all embarked on individual pilgrimages, be they 'real' ones – geographical displacement seems to be a way to construct one's identity – or more radical journeys, like Godfrey Rainbird's into the realm of death or inner ones such as Vera's. All these characters suffer from isolation, exclusion, illness, and their deaths form the climax of the narratives. But all of them have tried to do, or to be, something despite, or because, of their ordinariness. This is the link with the last three novels – *Daughter Buffalo*, *Living in the Maniototo*, and *The Carpathians* – where the figures of artists are more prominent and may be more promising: old Turnlung and Alice Pansy Proudlock are writers, and so too is John Henry Brecon in *The Carpathians*. But the main and most successful of these figures is no doubt Janet Frame herself, the arch-creator.

THE EDGE OF THE ALPHABET OR 'THE ALPHABET OF THE EDGE'?

In *The Edge of the Alphabet* Janet Frame tackles the topic of creativity, language and isolation. Thora Pattern is the narrator who organizes the narrative and the lives of her fictional characters. Her family name, Pattern, 'carries the connotations of mapmaking and selective point of view'.[2] She is Frame's spokes(wo)man, and stages the inadequacy of communication leading to isolation and despair and sometimes, as in the case of Zoe, even to suicide. The main topic of the book is exclusion in ordinary circumstances. The narrator depicts the hell of the ordinary: all the characters in the book are ordinary and live in ordinary circumstances. Jan Cronin insists on the difficulty there is in summarizing a novel that, 'in addition to patterning, seems in equal measure concerned with agency, alienation, apocalypse, art, authenticity, communication, death, dream, fiction, identity, individuality, language, marginality, meaning, memory, metafiction, migrancy, perception and the past'.[3] I argue that all Frame's novels could be said to be concerned with the same range of topics, which seems to render any attempt at analyzing them doomed from the start.

The three fictional characters that embark on a journey for the Continent are the New Zealander Toby Withers, Zoe Bryce from the Midlands and the Irishman Pat Keenan. Toby Withers' epilepsy is the main cause of his ostracization. He is another odd man out. Zoe presents another alternative: she is a spinster, a sort of double of Malfred in *A Stage of Siege* or of the Miss Edge/worth (my slash) Toby remembers in a burst of nostalgic homesickness: 'for years Miss Edgeworth had looked after her mother' (*EA* 147). Zoe manages to create a beautiful albeit insignificant silver figure, just before committing suicide. We may well surmise with Gina Mercer that Thora might also have committed suicide, if we refer to the prologue, where it seems that Peter Heron, the secondary character mentioned both in the pre-textual note and at the end of the novel, has found some of her notes after her death. In literary (Barthesian) criticism, this might be analysed in terms of the literal/symbolical death of the author and his author/ity: 'The publication of Thora's work necessitates her death'.[4] Frame deconstructs the conventional forms of the novel by inserting a 'visible' narrator, who is on a par with the characters, though (s)he also treats them as such: 'Do I, Thora Pattern, imagine that I can purchase people out of my fund of loneliness and place them like goldfish in the aquarium of my mind's room and there watch them day and night swimming round and round kept alive by the titbits which I feed to them' (*EA* 143). Thora merges with the characters who, like Alice/Mavis/Pansy in *Living in the Maniototo* are multiselved, as if they were meant to illustrate Frame's puzzling declaration in the Autobiography: 'I've created "selves" but I have never written of "me"' (III 154). The book is divided into three parts: the first deals with Toby's story, whose departure is triggered by his mother's death, as is often the case either in the novels (*A State of Siege*) or in the Autobiography. Bob and Toby are left alone together and Toby plans to go overseas like Janet before him, reiterating the quest of the Pakehas together with a more personal dream to see more of the world, to broaden his horizons.

We can perceive strong links between life and writing, *bio* and *graphy*. In *Wrestling With The Angel*, King relates Geordie Frame's trip to the Continent, his fit in Belgium and his consequent repatriation in New Zealand: 'And she was to make sympathetic use of some of Geordie's experience in [...] *The Edge of the Alphabet*' (*WA* 175). Toby Withers, the anti-hero, is a replica of his homonym in *Owls Do Cry*, himself a barely disguised fictionalization of Bruddie/Robert, Frame's epileptic brother. Alice Braun considers Toby as one of the most fascinating characters in Frame's fiction, because of his extraordinary ordinariness. The very title refers to those who do not belong, the cast-offs, those who are forever denied a voice or a history or those with whom the novels are peopled (I am referring to Milly Galbraith in *Intensive Care* or Decima in *The Carpathians*). But the title could also be easily transformed into its opposite as an example of antimetabole: 'the alphabet of the edge', reserved to those who do not speak the same language because they are different or those who will not speak at all, like Erlene/Vera in *Scented Gardens for the Blind* or Decima, the autistic (*oughtistick* as Milly would say in *Intensive Care*) girl in *The Carpathians*, who 'has no words' (*Ca* 106). These characters cannot but be seen in the light of Frame's tragic experience of difference. Toby's dream is to write a book – *The Lost Tribe* – though he is barely literate. Even the writing of a letter to his father proves a very laborious task, something which Miss Botting (the censorious teacher in the Autobiography) had not forewarned him of: 'The teacher had never told him that words were like this' (*EA* 74). At a party on board, he plays the part of Orpheus, but he has not the slightest idea who Orpheus might be and his guesses are almost comic: 'How can I be expected to know about Orpheus when I left school early [...] I do not think he is a Hollywood film star. Is he from the Bible? [...] Perhaps his wife was turned into a pillar of salt? My mother said to me, 'Never look back and never open forbidden doors and boxes'. But was not Orpheus a musician? In a jazz band? On the air? With harp, lute, guitar, organ' (*EA* 82). Michael King relates one of Geordie's visits to his sister in London, when he brought her 'a sheaf of handwritten manuscript pages, unpunctuated and full of misspellings, on which he was writing the story of his life' (*WA* 174).

Toby is as lost as the tribe he means to write about. But he is very possessive with regard to this 'never-to-be-written' book: '*The Lost Tribe*. No one but himself knew or understood the real meaning of it; no one possessed the subject as he did, and no one must ever share it' (*EA* 26). In her article, Jan Cronin analyses Toby's attitude in terms of 'the text's pervasive fear of inclusion and communion as a form of erasure',[5] which is the dilemma that most of Frame's characters experience: integration might entail the loss of one's integrity. The book will never be written, despite his mother's remembered and treasured creed that he may be a genius in disguise, another Julius Caesar whose epilepsy was a sure sign of his genius. In the Autobiography, Janet shows how much this theory has deeply influenced her attitude towards her illness, to the point that she wore it with the pride of one whose difference should not be dismissed or scorned, but valued and recognized. Toby, however, is no Janet, even though they have similar itineraries. They both embark on a sea trip after their mothers' deaths (Delrez sees Toby's mother's role as essential) as if geographical displacement was a sure way to reconstruct an unstable deconstructed self. The trope of the journey, which in a way inscribes Frame in a postcolonial tradition, is what structures her fiction and Autobiography. In *A State of Siege*, Malfred also leaves her native place after her mother's death. Like his homonym in *Owls Do Cry*, Toby has been rejected by Evelina on account of his illness. He has a fit on the boat and Pat helps him recover from it, taking possession of him, as he would like to do with Zoe (whose possessions he will look after, after her death) hoping, in true 'Patrick Reilly style' that she is 'fancy-free' (*EA* 141). As in the Autobiography, Pat gives advice to her about sex, which is more an attempt at trying to dissuade her from having any. Pat is the other male figure in *The Edge of the Alphabet*, a faithful replica of Patrick Reilly, the ridiculous Irishman Janet meets in London, her 'conformist New Zealand conscience' (III 105) or another Ted, the hero of the short story 'The Advocate', who is always on the side of the authorities, who does the right things at the right times, like Chicks in *Owls Do Cry*. Intertextual echoes are legion. 'The brief dream [he has] encapsulates Pat's dismal but ordinary life. He is unable to strike the match which might provide him with warmth, life, passion and risk' (*SF* 58). As in *Owls Do Cry*, too, Toby stands as a figure of in-betweenness. He vacillates between the two antagonistic poles of conformism – Pat on the one hand, and the aesthetic aspirations embodied by Zoe on the other, herself another Malfred. The two women are old maids, former teachers, who both leave their respective countries in a desperate quest for something new or 'simply' for meaning. Zoe is kissed on the boat and though the kisser is no romantic hero – 'a member of the crew, dark, unshaven, wearing a striped jersey' (*EA*, 104–105) – the moment is remembered as every first-time should be. It becomes 'the core of my life [...] my meaning' (*EA* 239). But 'There are too many dimensions' (*EA* 251) to this kiss, which makes it impossible to ascribe a specific meaning to it. For her travelling companions, their arrival in London is as disappointing as it is for Janet in the Autobiography where she confronts the drama of arrival. Great Britain is far from being the home Toby's father (and Janet's) had dreamt of. As an echo to the beginning of the third volume of the Autobiography, part three is devoted to London, its bleakness and inhospitality. Like Janet again, Toby is betrayed by the language, the discrepancy between signifier and signified when he is looking for a non-existent circus at Piccadilly. If the episode verges on the comic, since it does not have any serious consequences, it also reveals the gap between the two countries and on a larger scale, the universal problem of communication.

The three characters lead quite isolated and miserable lives. Toby develops a tumour on his arm, that feels 'like *tribal* fighting, in areas of his body' (*EA* 249; italics mine). For Delrez 'the throbbing pain accompanies the fight involved in writing about the Lost Tribe' (*MU* 59). But he can neither bring it into textual existence, nor will the wound be cured. As for Zoe, after creating an insignificant but much admired paper figure – as if it was only before death that such perfection and beauty could be attained – she commits suicide. Toby goes back to New Zealand to nurse an old aunt. 'This return signals the death of his ambitions, the death of the secret part of himself which he has longed to express' (*SF* 61) which might be imprisoned in his body, like a poison, unable to come out (*EA* 258).

A STATE OF SIEGE – PRISON OR FREEDOM?

After her parents' death, Malfred, an unmarried middle-aged art teacher decides to move from her native south to settle in the paradisical northern island of Karemoana where everything reaches an intensity unknown in the south: 'an island where storms were stormier, rain was rainier, sun was sunnier' (*SoS* 3). Malfred makes a move from south to north, from a past synonymous with illness, death and stagnation, to a present that should mean a new life, a new perspective. The island, however, is more a place of death than life. As Delrez convincingly argues, 'The island itself strikes Malfred as a kind of Hades, a no-man's land of experience on the outskirts of living' (*MU* 139), a reminder of psychiatric hospitals where the unwanted of this world are sent: '*Decrepit* was the word. Am I like that too? [...] Have I really come here like a worn-out elephant or those animals that hide when they are lame or sick, to die' (*SoS* 101; JF's italics). In *Intensive Care*, Frame's frightful dystopia, HADES is, ironically enough, a new acronym for Human Animal Decision Enquiry Services (*IC* 339). The previous owner of the house that Malfred has bought has herself died a mysterious death that cannot but anticipate her own. So that her choice of a place to which to retire might mean intensified petrification rather than an opening to the New View she aspires to: 'a trap is also a refuge' (II 96). Or vice versa.

As an art teacher she had specialized in the study of shadows at which she was said to be excellent. Like Toby's mother in *The Edge of the Alphabet*, Malfred's kept praising her for her rare talent at rendering shadows, as if it were a sufficient protection against any form of danger. As the only single member of the family – both her brother Graham and her sister Lucy are happily married – Malfred spent months looking after her dying mother, as if it were her privilege as an unmarried woman. In the Autobiography, Janet's family reproaches her with her going away, leaving her father alone. As the unmarried daughter it was her duty, they thought, to look after him: 'Malfred's relatives [...] appeal to her "strong sense of family responsibility"' (*MU* 137). Leaving her native place also means acquiring the independence she has never had since she was only her father's 'daughter' (*SoS* 6), an argument her friends and relatives use to try and deter her from leaving home. The choice of insularity is a guarantee of isolation: 'Small are islands, a tyranny of completeness' (III 66). Simone Oettli-van Delden endorses Susan Ash's[6] argument that Malfred means to avoid any human contact, thereby adopting the artist's cliché stance. In the third volume of the Autobiography, Janet rejects El Vici Mario's proposal since it would mean staying in Andorra, raising a family and giving up her writing. Though I partly agree with Ash's view, I would rather see Malfred as looking not so much for isolation (she desperately wants access to a telephone) as for 'the New Vision' she repeatedly alludes to, even if it all ends up in death: 'Death was a cold touch to be used for release into Life' (*SoS* 47). Such isolation of course is often regarded as the necessary pre-condition for creation. She now leaves behind her place, her people, her old vision: 'The New View thus emerges as a reaction to the rigidities of realistic representation' (*MU* 143). Malfred's paintings had always been praised for their life-likeness. What she now paints is different, using lanolin as she had done for her dying mother: 'it is worth noticing that the finished picture departs from the more realistic manner typical of Malfred's earlier marinescapes' (*MU* 141). She is embracing her new vision, even if the embrace might prove fatal.

Throughout her life, Janet-like Malfred has abided by the laws, both in her personal life and in her drawing, to the point that she treated her pupils with a severity dictated by this belief in the power of the norm: 'She remembered, now, the fear she had known at the sight of the leaf and seed not completely imprisoned in a firmly defined BB boundary' (*SoS* 73). Frame used to think that grammatical mistakes were a mortal sin. Conversely, Malfred resented those who, like Lettice, showed a creative talent far superior to hers: 'she had been awed by it, had been envious of it and of the *secret store* from which Lettice had drawn her knowledge and understanding of times that she had never experienced' (*SoS* 122; italics mine). In the Autobiography, Janet desperately wants to be praised for her imagination, a talent some of her school-friends seem to possess more abundantly than she does. It is actually for her lack of it that Malfred despised her sister Lucy, the 'giggling school girl' (*SoS* 129) (another facet of young Janet), whom she later briefly hallucinates into a (un)likely prowler. Lucy is a replica of Chicks in *Owls Do Cry*, or Greta in *The Adaptable Man*, the perfect housewife who charms people into reading the mediocre books she herself chooses. Malfred's frustrations are inscribed on her face in the form of two lines, signalling her spinsterhood. All her life, every month of it, she has prepared herself 'for the great moment' (*SoS* 77) which never came, but the desire has never completely receded. In her article on '*A State of Siege* le langage du trou',[7] Alice Braun focuses on Malfred's body, on her skin that is as much a protection of her as the walls of her house: 'Only Malfred's skin, taut against her flesh, took over the role played by wood, glass, iron, as defensive inviolable membrane' (*SoS* 79).

Even her clothes are in character. She wears 'a brown costume' (*SoS* 219), that is either 'old-fashioned' or 'subtle', depending on the perspective. At 53, Malfred has known love only once and that was with Wilfred who died in the war. In her stream of reminiscences, she relates two different versions of her sexual encounter with him which testifies, as it might be, to the relativity of truth, autobiographical or fictional. In the first version, they meet in the fernhouse and she resents the kiss he gives her, which both frightens and disgusts her. Wilfred's death, a month later, is paralleled by the destruction of the fernhouse. As for Janet, who had her first sexual encounter aged 33 with the American Bernard/Parlette, she feels that all exits are blocked: 'I knew or felt that I was as sexless as a block of wood' (III 74). If Wilfred was the intruder, Malfred knows that she wouldn't let him enter. Malfred fears the intrusion of an 'other' who could violate her privacy. Inside the house, she is fascinated by a hole in the ceiling: 'The light curved, mellow, upon the ceiling, directing itself upon the wound where the light fitting had been' (*SoS* 88), which reminds her of the old woman in hospital who had 'a small dark red hole with raw edges' (*SoS* 88). This raw wound from which part of the self could escape was a source of fear for Malfred who is both obsessed with control and containment and also fascinated by the possibilities afforded by the aperture. As for the intruder, whether 'visitor or guest' (*SoS* 79), she wavers between the two opposing feelings of fear and pleasure.

The knocking has become a familiar part of her surroundings and maybe even of her life; she is no longer alone. And when it briefly stops, the ensuing silence is 'tyrannical, cunning' (*SoS* 161) in its absoluteness. On the fifth day of her stay, Malfred hears once more a frightful, almost incessant knocking on the door, a proleptic echo of the invisible presence in Mattina Brecon's room in *The Carpathians*. She first attributes the knocking to an indefinite paranoid 'they' (*SoS* 80), before trying to give the intruder a more precise identity. Malfred tries several strategies – from speaking out loud, in the hope of frightening it away, to threatening to call the police. That is when she discovers that the phone is unplugged: 'the phone was attached to a useless length of cord, connected to nothing, and she was alone again, besieged in the dark with no help' (*SoS* 99). But she persists in pretending she is talking to the doctor and the priest.

In the third and last part of the book, entitled 'The Stone', Malfred imagines a succession of hypothetical intruders, ranging from her parents to her sister, brother and Wilfred, recalling to her images of the past, of her relationship with her family. And she remembers a generous father, whom she saw in another light through his relation with other people and a predatory mother whose ordinariness she resented as much as Janet despised her parents for not sharing her intellectual life. She also remembers a more fulfilling sexual encounter with Wilfred: 'we made love in the fernhouse, and I did not, as I need to remember that I did, turn Wilfred away or mock him but I loved him with my body and with my thoughts' (*SoS* 205–6). Malfred rejects the usual clichés that Janet is very much aware of in her own love affair with the American Bernard: 'One does not need war to help spill platitudes!' (*SoS* 208).

In the end, Malfred is found dead clutching a stone wrapped up in a piece of paper with 'Help' written on it (an echo to her own previous calls), followed by a nonsense poem, which reminds one not only of *Alice's Adventures* or Jabberwocky but also of Godfrey Rainbird's icy spelling, Vera's primitive cry or Milly's phonetic spelling or some nonsense poems. It is a new language that is both opaque and creative as it culminates in the promise of the Sun. Mark Delrez speaks of linguistic utopianism. This puzzling ending has given rise to a number of interpretations.[8] But as Cronin percipiently concludes in her article: 'In initiating an interaction between him/her-self and a potentially inviolable context, the reader then consciously or unconsciously confronts the limitations of his own interpretive system'.[9]

Like Zoe, in *The Edge of the Alphabet*, Malfred has had access to beauty and to this new language but it is only at the cost of her own life, as if the revelation had been too much: 'a record of imaginative failure' (*MU* 150). Delrez places Malfred in the category of the 'unworthy visionaries', like Toby Withers or Edward Glace, 'who finally fail to capitalize on their special talents' (*MU* 149). But I would argue that what matters more is not the outcome, but rather the effort that has gone into achieving it. In this sense, Malfred's is perhaps the triumph of failure.

SCENTED GARDENS FOR THE BLIND OR THE MOCK TRINITY

As for *Scented Gardens for the Blind*, Marc Delrez considers it the most difficult, or as Simone Oettli-van Delden puts it, 'the most accomplished novel'.[10] It is certainly one of the most destabilizing, the least 'Heimlich' of Frame's fiction. The three voices we hear are those of the three members of the Glace family – Vera's, the mother's, Erlene's (the daughter who has willed herself mute), and Edward's (the father). The latter has exiled himself in Great Britain and become obsessed with genealogical research and in one family in particular, the Strangs (Strong, Strange, Strangle?). It is as though there are three possible ways of living, or three dead ends. Each of them is given equal textual space (five chapters each). Each of them lives in a separate world, once more illustrating Frame's notion of impossible communication. In her article, Jeanne Delbaere uses the eloquent and convincing expression: 'barricaded self'.[11] Nonetheless, they all try to break out of this isolation in some way or other – Vera by begging her daughter to speak, Edward by trying to uncover an unknown family's hidden secrets, and Erlene by choosing a blackbeetle as a confidant whom she calls Uncle.

The beetle's own story and even his cousin's are embedded in the main narrative as if to reflect Edward's quest. Cousin Albert (Camus?) Blackbeetle had waited all his life, Sisyphus-like, for a ball of dung, to come miraculously his way to help him build his own house: 'The story of Albert Dungbeetle can be seen as a reduced and negative version of Albert Camus's Myth of

Sisyphus'.[12] No ball was big enough for him, but when the desirable object of desire finally fell from heaven, he managed with great efforts to drag it to the place where all his family had died of hunger and exhaustion after their years of waiting. The ball, however, was so huge that it blocked the entrance and Albert ended up buried alive. Albert Blackbeetle's life is a parable-like parody of Edward's; their two hubristic quests are doomed. Erlene's blackbeetle friend acts as counterpart to Dr Clapper – the name is highly significant – who plays the part of Erlene's therapist by trying to make her speak. As father figures, the two are sometimes confused with one another. The blackbeetle claims that he is indeed Dr Clapper (*SGB* 190), though his frown indicates he is not so sure about his identity. The confusion includes Edward as well in a reproduction of the narrative trinity staged in the novel. In the above-mentioned exchange about their identities, the blackbeetle resorts to the hackneyed phrases which Frame never misses an opportunity to denounce and ridicule.

Her aim is to take issue with a sterile, petrified language and to create something new. Delrez argues that if the endings of the novels are often apocalyptic (as in *The Carpathians*) or deeply pessimistic, we should not however miss the point of what he calls 'the remedial (etiological?) dimension' of her fiction (*MU* 124; my parenthesis). Only at the very end of the book do we discover that we have been manipulated, plunged from the beginning into a schizophrenic mind, since it is only then that we learn there is but one character: Vera, who has spent thirty years in a mental hospital and who has never uttered a word since, and 'has created herself as a family' (*SF* 77); we could readily argue that hers is a highly dysfunctional family with an absent husband whose only interest is in other 'strange' families, and with a daughter who refuses to speak to the point that Vera slaps her in exasperation: 'Her mother struck her across her face, pressing her lip across her teeth so that her lip was pierced and the blood trickled down the corner of her mouth' (*SGB* 192). It is blood that issues from the organ of speech instead of the desired words, an echo to the invasive blood of the beginning: 'I hear blood [...] the first sound was blood [...] the gossiping blood [...] the terrible babbling of blood [...] the tell-tale demands of my blood' (*SGB* 21).

What terrifies silent Vera is the possible contamination of silence, as if it were an illness, though as Gina Mercer convincingly argues, silence also means a form of power, of protest, of resistance, a refusal to play the game, to be like the others: 'But Change says nothing; he too knows that his power lies in his silence' (*SGB* 213). Vera has gone as far as to will herself blind (which is altogether both frightening and also reassuring for her) as an answer to 'their' useless phrases of consolation: 'At least there is consolation in knowing she is not blind' (*SGB* 14). 'Vera resorts to blindness as an attempt to tap a fund of alternative vision' (*MU* 142). As Oettli-van Delden argues, Vera could be a variant of Frame herself as her ambivalence towards illness shows: blindness or silence, like schizophrenia, could be a protective skin against a judgmental world. In the Autobiography, Frame says that she was at a loss when the diagnosis of schizophrenia was overturned in London, and that she felt, so to speak like a 'skinned rabbit' (I 171). For what Vera also most fears is the judgement of others, of being found responsible for her daughter's refusal to speak, which she both pities and resents. Oettli-van Delden argues that 'silence is thus grounded in childhood',[13] and she quotes the opening page of the novel that illustrates one of the unobtrusive though unmistakable autobiographical elements: 'And whenever Poppy and I met, we talked and talked, because we were friends. But if by chance in our walking [...], we got out of step or we separated [...] the curse of silence was put upon us. [...] And we shut our mouths tight, [...] only stared at each other, judging, judging, and I could see my crimes like clear glittering pictures in Poppy's eyes' (*SGB* 9–10).

Edward's genealogical research is certainly a remedy for the existential anxiety in him, that finds vent in his decision to build himself a perfect chair: 'It seemed to Edward that he needed desperately and immediately a material impartial object to contain him' (*SGB* 200), a source of comfort and security. Though at the time of Vera's blindness, chairs had turned into enemies: 'the chair habitually submissive, close to love and death and the bad smells of the human body; in and out of fashion. The chairs in our house are tall-backed, with bars, and webbing beneath the seat, [...] these are kitchen chairs; red with blood; submit, submit, torture, leveled secrets, primitive disclosures;

dark-brown chairs stained with people' (*SGB* 18–19). No wonder Edward is 'chair-obsessed'. But the perfect chair cannot fit Edward's imperfect body; the dream cannot really come true. The chair seems to fit Vera better, since at the end, she is sitting on a chair 'looking human' (*SGB* 251), as if the chair had the magical power to restore a lost dignity, to give back to Vera her human status. The only contact Vera has in the hospital is with one Clara Strang. She coincidentally bears the same name as the last of the Strangs Edward had paid a visit to, a foster mother to three orphans who are terrified of her. That Clara Strang questions Edward's right to pry into their family lives, as one of the other Strangs had done, taking Edward for a sort of peddlar as Janet's mother does in the Autobiography with the doctor who is coming to deliver the news of Myrtle's death.

Gina Mercer sees Edward as the embodiment of the past whereas Vera would be the present and Erlene the future. Edward's obsessive passion leads him to intrude upon a reluctant family to discover their secrets, as if discovering someone else's secrets should be one's aim in life: 'I know, Erlene thought. You want to torture it out of me' (*SGB* 193). Vera's desperate attempts to discern the reasons for her daughter's refusal to speak end in failure. Even the aptly-named Dr Clapper (who tries to cajole Erlene into speaking by confessing he 'feels the same way' as she does (*SGB* 170) in an echo to the doctor's strategy in *Faces in the Water*) enjoys no success on that front. 'The odds are high, then, that the form of speech taught by Dr Clapper would resemble the logorrhea which Vera set out to discard in the first place, and thus may not, in itself, represent a positive alternative to her silence' (*MU* 103).

Vera's name assumes its full significance at the end of the book. That is when a sort of verity emerges, that Vera is the sole narrator. But is it the truth? And if so, which one? At the beginning of the text, Vera ponders about truth: 'Truth may be a vast ocean within reach of all but how genuine are truths that have been drawn from the ocean, distilled, bottled, flavored, diluted, chilled, boiled, in fact adulterated with the potion of ourselves?' (*SGB* 39). She then goes on to illustrate the relativity of truth as regards Edward's physical appearance: 'Edward is a dark-haired man wearing dark-rimmed spectacles. Edward is a balding man wearing rimless mirror-like spectacles. Both are true, if one removes the adulteration of time' (*SGB* 39). At the end, Vera has rid herself of the conventional language of clichés. Hers is a 'prelinguistic form of vague mutter' (*MU* 123), a primitive cry, an animal grunt, 'out of ice and stone' (*SGB* 252). But it is at least authentic. It is what Dr Clapper recognizes at last as 'the language of humanity' (*SGB* 251), as if this gift had come with the total eradication of Great Britain, a *tabula rasa* that anticipates the cataclysmic shower of letters in *The Carpathians*. We can wonder with Delbaere whether this is an end or a new beginning, whether this kind of new way of speaking is as cold and petrified as the stone and ice it comes from, or if it is a promise of creation, 'Whether Vera Glace's oracular message [...] is an end or a new beginning is not for me to decide'.[14] Frame believes in the right to choose; no option should be more valid than the other. She rejects the rigid binary system of thought that leads to the exclusion and condemnation of those who are not on the 'right' side: 'And so we have grouped the deaf, dumb, blind, crippled, mentally ill, in one mass in order to "deal with" them, for we must "deal with" these vast surfaces of strangeness which demand all our lives a protective varnish of sympathy' (*SGB* 14).

The final twist anticipates the last novel, *The Carpathians*, where we learn that John Henry is an orphan and that he is, like Turnlung in *Daughter Buffalo*, the sole writer of the story we have been reading.

THE RAINBIRDS OR *YELLOW FLOWERS IN THE ANTIPODEAN ROOM*

Janet Frame wanted to change the first title into the second, against her publishers W. H. Allen's and Albion Wright's advice, who 'also held out against *Yellow Flowers* [...] Georges Braziller [...] gave priority to his author's wishes and duly published the Dunedin novel [...] as *Yellow Flowers in the Antipodean Room* [...] creating a source of confusion for future bibliographers and critics' (*WA* 331).

Gina Mercer stresses the fact that it was written after Frame's return to New Zealand from her seven-year exile. Whereas she had gone away as the 'mad niece', she returns as a successful, prestigious writer, the prodigal Janet. *The Rainbirds* is her seventh novel. Like Zoe, Godfrey has emigrated from Great Britain to New Zealand after his parents' death in one of the explosions that so often happen in Frame's fiction. He has left behind him an unmarried sister, Lynley, who runs a boarding-house. In New Zealand he marries Beatrice and they have two kids; he works as a clerk in a tourist office. Their life is the picture of normality, until he is run over by a car and declared dead. Everything is ready for his funeral. His sister flies to New Zealand where she even plans to settle for good when, to everybody's amazement, Godfrey comes back from the dead. The rest of the novel hinges on the unanimous reaction to the unbelievable, inconceivable, fact of his resurrection. They all hold it against him. He loses his job, his friends, his children, and finally his wife before dying for good himself. Resurrection only happens once.

Godfrey's is another sort of journey, a more radical one. His is a reversed kind of exile as he leaves 'home' (the usual name for Great Britain) to settle in the dominion: 'He chose New Zealand as a home' (*Ra* 3). He was the perfect candidate for emigration to New Zealand, like Zita, the young Hungarian woman and her family in *Living in the Maniototo*: 'EUROPEAN OF British birth, twenty, single, not a convicted criminal, not suffering from physical or mental illness, politically placid, beardless, Godfrey Rainbird was well qualified to be accepted as an assisted immigrant to New Zealand' (*Ra* 3; Janet Frame's capitals). He has already had a taste of New Zealand's xenophobia on his arrival, for it turns out that the cemetery is reserved to the natives or those who have lived long enough in the place. But that is nothing in comparison with what is in store for him after his resurrection.

Beatrice, his wife, is a subdued replica of Chicks in *Owls Do Cry*, in her wish to adapt, to conform, to read the right books: 'She could quote French verbs and Latin mnemonics. She had read *Wuthering Heights*' (*Ra* 6). And she also shares with Chicks or Janet's mother her taste for clichés: 'Borrowed thoughts and judgments conserved energy' (*Ra* 122). Conformism is indeed comfort. What characterizes Beatrice is also her need for reassuring possessions, Godfrey being one of them. There is actually a fight over Godfrey between his wife and his sister. Lynley, who had come prepared to (re)claim dead Godfrey as hers (dead bodies are often claimed and reclaimed in Frame's fiction) and 'preside over his burial' (*Ra* 48) feels utterly dispossessed when the burial is cancelled for lack of a body. Godfrey himself, after his resurrection, clings to his family in an almost child-like way, rendered through the accumulative style Frame uses in her short stories where the narrators are often children: 'to hold fast to his wife *and* children *and* house *and* garden *and* lawn *and* tools' (*Ra* 89; italics mine). When he is officially declared alive again, Beatrice is torn between her joy at seeing him alive and her embarrassment at having to cancel all the arrangements for the funeral (she actually keeps the coffin she has already paid for), at having to tell the friends and neighbours and Godfrey's sister. The neighbours' sympathy for the bereaved woman is expressed with the usual clichés: 'Bear up' (which is a direct echo to the words of consolation in 'Keel and Kool'). The neighbours' name, Todds, is also the family's name in 'Keel and Kool', and it may be no coincidence that Tod means death in German.

Godfrey's death had given him an aura that extended to his wife and children, which Beatrice expresses in an almost comic way: 'Now let me enjoy his death' (*Ra* 27). Once he is no longer dead, not only does that aura vanish, but it leaves her with a sense of resentment and bitterness at having been cheated: '[He] should have stayed dead' (*Ra* 181). The 'marvel', the 'miracle' becomes a 'monster' as Godfrey has usurped his prerogatives and transgressed the ways of the dead; once dead, always dead. In the Autobiography, Frame insists – almost *ad absurdum* – on the prestige that the death of a close relative confers, regretting that it is 'only' her sister that has died, which is not enough to 'qualify', though she later revises this in *Daughter Buffalo* where Turnlung relates the interest aroused by the death of the sister of a friend of his. Godfrey's coming back to life is felt as a universal betrayal. He is now seen as a criminal who has dared to come back to the scene of crime, or a freak, the ('Ole Cripply Rainbird' (*Ra* 218)) or even a mad man. He is now dis-qualified for life. Ostracization first takes the form of indifference, then of verbal and physical violence. Rumours circulate about the family and the children are officially taken away to their aunt Lynley's who has settled in Auckland. Stones are thrown at him as if he were a male version of the adulterous Mary Magdalen, with death for a mistress. 'Through this parable-like story, it is at New Zealand that Frame throws stones to denounce its exacerbated conformism, its intolerance and xenophobia. 'She has taken it upon herself, after her return from overseas, to throw a few satirical stones at Dunedin culture.' (*SF* 151)

Godfrey has had the privilege of exploring a world nobody has ever had access to, or at least one from which nobody has ever been able to return. People may be envious: 'Godfrey detected the envious note in his voice' (*Ra* 57). Above all they are terrified: 'the look of horror [...] horrified' (*Ra* 54) because he has become so different that nobody dares to approach him out of superstition (*Ra* 139). It is as if he were suffering from an unknown infectious disease, or a handicap, as his future employer tells him, to justify his firing him. Death has brought with it a terrible division within the couple, materialized by Godfrey's cold, stiff body: 'as if you have been turned to stone' (*Ra* 91). He cannot manage to warm it up and he has even become 'impervious to sunlight' (*Ra* 98), badly needing that coat which Beatrice has already given to her own father. Godfrey is being dispossessed, both of his former life, and of his death. The embedded story of the woman who was diagnosed terminally ill and who recovered, is significant: on hearing that she would not die, as she had been led to expect, she committed suicide. This fictional story is not unlike Janet's real one in which, when told she had never suffered from schizophrenia, felt like a skinned rabbit precisely because her illness had become a kind of protective second skin. But as for Janet, Godfrey's plea also helps him discover another world, another level of experience, epitomized by his 'icy spelling', a dyslexia born from his extraordinary experience of death, which gives him just as extraordinary a visionary power (could we read a pun in the 'icy'/'I see' spelling?), the prerogative of those who are different, albeit this new power only increases his difference and his solitude. Nobody can share in an experience that has had only one example in (religious) history. Godfrey's resurrection takes place three days after his death, and he is about Christ's age. Refusing a job as a lift attendant, he stays at home repairing electrical appliances, but cutting himself off more and more from a world that more and more rejects him in a kind of inescapable and inevitable vicious circle.

Throughout her work, Frame denounces the taboo of death, when the subject is either not mentioned or euphemized; the mother never utters the word 'dead' or 'died', either in the Autobiography, in the short story 'Keel and Kool', or 'The Secret', fearing, as it were, its performative power. The climax of this 'strategy of avoidance' is the other short story 'The Mythmaker' where Frame depicts a totalitarian regime in which the word as well as the thing are forbidden. Death must not be seen (this is a recurrent motif in the short story 'Snowman, Snowman', in *Daughter Buffalo* or in *Intensive Care*): 'This hasty dispatch was unseemly, a Christian urge to put the dead out of sight, concealing the body while pretending one could draw comfort from the hovering immortal soul, when the only comfort was that of improved hygiene!' (*Ra* 36).

Thirty-five years later Sonny and Teena, the Rainbirds' children, return, the first as a town clerk and the second as an actress. Ironically enough, Godfrey's story has become a legend, attracting the tourists he used to work for: 'fair's fair' (*Ra* 138).

THE ADAPTABLE MAN – ADAPT OR PERISH

The Adaptable Man has its genesis in a visit the previous year to a dentist in Camberwell:

> His consulting room looked so old and everything was frayed [...] It seemed like something out of the past. And so I wrote about a dentist... I wrote the book around him as I imagined him... [I] quite enjoy imagining lives for people whom I see only once or twice and don't know. (*WA* 241) (ellipses, Janet Frame's)

Unity Foreman, the witch novelist, as she calls herself – and the metaphor runs from beginning to end – is modelled on Thora Pattern (or Mavis or John Henry Brecon), but she is more of a journalist than a writer. Her name is highly ironical for what the community of Little Burgelstatham, located in Suffolk (where Janet herself spent some time writing when she was in England), lacks is precisely a sense of unity. The list of individual 'I's' in the prologue – which opens with a Shakespearean mock prophecy and ends on a list of five 'I's' – (*AM* 7) sets the tone. The myth of the community is debunked from the start as the town is more an amalgam of different individualities, a gallery of portraits, than a coherent whole (*SF* 90). The name of the town itself links it to death: 'a *burgel* was originally a burial place of the heathen' (*AM* 12). Greta Maude feels buried alive in the place, reproaching her husband with having refused to make a career and settle in town. Each of the ten chapters that follow the prologue and constitute the first part is devoted to the characters that have been introduced. The Maudes are a family of three: Russell, the father, is an old-fashioned dentist and stamp-collector, his wife Greta, a staunch adept of gardening, and their son 'Alwyn' a student and a budding writer – he will end up as a journalist on his return from Spain – and the murderer of the foreigner El Botti Julio with whom the novel opens. The El Vici Mario of the Autobiography is, in fact, El Botti Mario (*WA* 168) who, like El Botti Julio, has been in a concentration camp. Russell's brother, Aisley, is a retired clergyman who is suffering from tuberculosis and a loss of faith. He is as old-fashioned, as unadaptable or unadapted as his brother; his impulse to *fly* back into the past echoed by Russell's fascination for planes.

After his death, Russell seems to have become his sibling: 'he had grown to resemble his brother Aisley, as if at Aisley's death, Russell had taken on the burden of being Aisley' (*AM* 276). Botti Julio, the foreigner, had learned a few – ridiculous – stock phrases (which are the title of the first part: 'These photographs are underexposed. Please will you intensify them' *AM* 9) to try to adapt to his new life in England where he has come to help with the black-currant harvest. His murder has no other reason than his being a foreigner: 'Dead exiles, expatriates, are always an embarrassment' (*AM* 64). The title of the book is thoroughly ironic. Alwyn is the adaptable man 'with a difference', in that he is all for stasis, that is unless 'stasis' is to be understood as a 'different' form of adaptation. Delrez underlines the similarity between his getting rid of unwelcome presences – 'Destruction gave him special happiness' (*AM* 62) – and Greta's abusive use of pesticides. Like mother, like son: both cultivate sameness and uniformity to the point that they have fleeting sexual intercourse in the garden shed, and Greta becomes pregnant. This dysfunctional community only functions with the exclusion of others, those who are perceived as intruders unless they conform in every respect: 'Stray thoughts were trimmed along with stray hair; brain-vines, tentacles of thought, were not encouraged to wander' (*AM* 3). Uniformity (the right haircut) might be the social equivalent of the medical lobotomy (the right 'brain-cut') Frame was about to undergo. This is probably the essential meaning of this novel, illustrating the author's more general concern with all those who are different in one way or another. At a more aesthetic level it is also, however, the denunciation of the dangers and limitations of strict realism that Frame has also highlighted in *A State of Siege*.

El Botti Julio's death does not cause the slightest stir in the village. 'Unity's report falsifies the story of Botti Julio' (*MU* 157) as though such an insignificant event does not matter. And indeed it does not: 'An Italian whom no one knew was of as little importance as the sixty-five passengers in the foreign plane lost over the Andes, or the inhabitants of the village buried by earthquake or avalanche' (*AM* 150). Some lives are worth more than others: 'Over Bombay or Bangkok or somewhere remote enough for the crash to be of little news value – unless the passengers are British, when, naturally, their age, appearance, profession, marital status and number of children will be announced' (*AM* 203). The only one who is concerned is Aisley, the former priest: '"To die", he said "so far from one's own country!"' (*AM* 59).

Greta is another Chicks, someone who used to take lessons in elocution, who prides herself on having a house 'situated in best part of' (*AM* 80), and who deplores her husband's lack of ambition. Though Russell is good at his job, his methods and instruments are as old-fashioned as the man himself. His interest in dentistry is accounted for by the fact that teeth endure, defying the power of time, like Russell himself, who is one of life's survivors. But dentistry is as unheroic and as colourless as he is, though Delrez sees him as the real hero in a novel that satirizes modernity at all costs when modernity or progress equate to dehumanization, careless killing, regress(ion). That is where I disagree with Karin Hansson about Frame's anti-Darwinism. To a certain degree, she is no doubt right. Yet what Frame denounces is rather a kind of ferocious, extreme technical progress, a materialism which entails a loss of contact with the natural world. At the same time, she denounces the immobilism of the villagers who are against any form of innovation. Electricity is seen as a demonic intruder, like the overspill Burgelstatham is threatened with, in an age where "genocide is the basis of survival"' (*AM* 149), and where homicide could be the first step towards it.

It is also very ironical that one of the only times when most of the community come together is at the end, as for the Last Supper, for what is to be their last night. Muriel Baldry has inherited a Venetian chandelier and invites her neighbours, the Maudes, for a 'chandelier hanging' party that ironically and cataclysmically ends in death for Aisley, Greta and Muriel when the chandelier comes smashing down on them. Her husband, Vic Baldry, survives but is paralysed, an emblem of the stasis the village is trapped in and from which he had always wanted to escape, 'living in a state of geographical bigamy' (*AM* 29): 'The marvel was, everyone said, that Vic Baldry had *adapted* himself to a smooth, weatherless world that he could not reach or touch – to his living his life in a mirror' (*AM* 277; italics mine). Karin Hansson legitimately wonders if his is an enviable fate, but she herself quotes Frame for an answer: 'For instance, this man who is totally paralysed in *The Adaptable Man* and views life through a mirror, I think that's a triumph'.[15] The only other survivor (apart from Alwyn who seems to have disappeared from the narration) ironically enough, is Russell, whose yearning for the past prevents him from adapting *ad absurdum*, to adopt 'the furious adaptation of his age' (*AM* 150). The unadaptable has proved the best adapted.

INTENSIVE CARE – 'HISTORY'/'HISTREE'/'HER/STORY'/'HER TREE'

The title is an obvious reference to the world of hospitals, with which the first part is concerned: 'she drew to some extent on the family story about her father falling in love with a nurse in the course of the First World War and her own stay in hospital in London the previous year' (*WA* 338).

At first sight, the three parts of this novel seem to form an incoherent whole. The first focuses on Tom Livingstone, a veteran from the First World War, the second on his grandson Colin and his tragic love affair, and the third, a hundred years later, on a dystopian world where people like Milly Galbraith are decimated (Milly's mother is called Decima, the name of the autistic girl in *Living in the Maniototo*). Gina Mercer sees this tripartite division along temporal lines: Past, Present and Future, with the seeds of violence contained in the first two quite logically developing into the frightful dystopia of the third. Delrez perceives another form of continuity between the three in the presence of the tree (Milly's 'histree' encompasses the tree and his/tory) as a controlling trope but also in the repetitive patterns or echoes: all the women – from Ciss to Peggy (first part), Lorna (second part) and Milly (third) – have striking violet eyes. '[T]he structure of the novel emphazises the notion of historical continuity, in that each of its three parts deals with the aftermath of a world war; while the text contains a number of clues suggesting that the third part, which is set in a post-holocaust New Zealand, directly follows from whatever seeds of discord were planted in the first two (*MU* 191). History influences his/story as best illustrated by Tom who (con)fuses Love and War: 'The Livingstones loved too much, like bombing' (*IC* 234).

In the first part, 'Kindness itself, Happiness itself, and Delphiniums', Tom is the main character, obsessed with his first love, Ciss Everest, the nurse who looked after him when he was wounded during the war. After his unloved wife's death (he dreamed that he had drowned her) he goes back to London, breaks his leg and is admitted to the hospital where coincidentally, the Ciss of his youth is dying. The woman of his dream 'In the dream, in the dream' (*IC* 1) – has become a tarted up old doll (who looks like the dressed-up mad patients in *Faces in the Water*), who wears 'a transformation' and fails to recognize him. In his rage and suffering, Tom smothers her under her pillow and flies back to New Zealand without further ado. This first part is interspersed with poetic letters from Naomi, Tom's daughter, whom Jeanne Delbaere compares to Daphne in *Owls Do Cry*, since she writes letters from the hospital where she is dying of cancer. On his return home, Tom meets Peggy Warren, the second violet-eyed woman, 'Miss Second World War' (*IC* 35), who gradually takes possession of his house and whom he is about to marry when he dies of a haemorrhage. Leonard, his brother, the 'black sheep of the family' (*IC* 59), also a veteran from the war, succeeds him and ends up in hospital where Peggy visits him before he dies on his return home.

It is through Pearl, Tom's other daughter, that the link between the two parts is established. She is the mother of Colin, the protagonist in the second part, who took up accountancy, like his homonym in the third part, Colin Monk. Pearl's is a huge invasive presence from which both her henpecked husband and her over-protected child wish to escape. Colin follows in his grandfather's footsteps, marries a woman he doesn't really love, has two children, and runs away with his young colleague Lorna, the third violet-eyed woman, with whom he lives a passionate but fleeting love story in Australia. When Lorna leaves him to obey her parents' wishes (but also her own), he cannot bear it and shoots the whole family and himself, to his mother's amazement, as he had been given 'everything an only son could have' (*IC* 198). Frame might have found inspiration for this character in her cousin Bill who did the same: 'Bill Frame, son of her Uncle Bill and Aunty Dolly, had shot his lover in Christchurch, killed her parents, then turned the rifle on himself' (*WA* 287). The second part of *Intensive Care* ends with Naomi's poetic farewell from the ironically named 'Recovery Unit' where the body of one of the patients, Miriam, has been dismembered and its different parts distributed among the others. The ironical refrain 'in the dream' echoes the very first line of the novel as the dream is but the nightmare of the third part, entitled: 'Pear Blossom to Feed the Nightmare'.

In his article, 'Janet Frame's Brave New World', Victor Dupont[16] focuses mainly on this last part, a Huxley-like dystopia, where the 'different', 'the deformed, the insane, the defective, the outcasts, the unhappy' (*IC* 342) are condemned by a euphemistic but just as efficient 'Human Delineation Act'. Milly Galbraith is the protagonist/narrator of this last part. She is the child-woman (whom people treat as a child) whose body and brain are diminutive, but whose 'different' intelligence enables her to have a clearer vision. It is Colin Monk, the mathematician (whose passion for 'clean' numbers tallies with the Government's need for cleanliness) who is entrusted with the duty of executing the general Classification plan which is based upon the elimination of memory and the radical eradication of the misfits. As in *Brave New World*, a new law replaces another without people being able to remember the first. The tranquillizers in the water supplies are 'expected to ward off [...] protest' (*IC* 215), to extinguish any incipient rebellion. Milly herself does not rebel, but patiently waits under the old Livingstone pear tree with Samuel the cat on her knees for the Decision Day, which coincides with her twenty-sixth birthday. As a presage of her fate, however, the tree will be felled because, according to Milly's father, it has become dangerous. The killing of the tree means the end of a time of happiness and protection for Milly, the beginning of the end. Milly's only friend is Sandy Monk, the Reconstructed Man she has constructed for herself, Colin Monk's fantasized twin, who knows what is in store for them. This new 'dim-mock-crissy' (*IC* 264) as Milly phonetically and maybe ironically calls the New State, is founded on the Nazi-influenced theory of processing and elimination, leaving only the happy few survivors, the fittest (as in *Living in the Maniototo*). They will then be the happier, without the unhappy, they will have more 'Lebensraum' and more ease, without the dis-eased, in this 'Friendly City of the South', that is supposed to set an example for the whole world, as even the 'A/merry/kins' come to help (*IC* 268; slashes added). The enterprise is like a gigantic spring-clean based on eugenics and euthanasia. The elderly people even plead for a merciful death before D-Day, though they desperately, physically, cling to life at the last moment. On D-Day, there will be a division of humans and animals (a reminder of the Alphas and Deltas or Epsilons in *Brave New World*), which leads parents to plead for their children, and offer 'bribe-berry'.

Milly's alphabet is phonetic, to the point that the reader has to make a particular effort at translating her long paratactic manuscript into the 'right' alphabet. Like Godfrey Rainbird, she has privileged access to the 'lining' of words. It is only at the end, after her and her parents' extermination, that her manuscript is found (as in Atwood's dystopian *The Handmaid's Tale*) and read by the incredulous authorities who are baffled that such a retarded person could have produced such an intelligent manuscript: 'How do you account for the intellectual grasp, the power of recall? This isn't the Milly Galbraith as described in the records' (*IC* 335). They may be as baffled as the doctors were when they discovered that Janet Frame had won a literary prize and that a lobotomy might not be necessary after all. But in this case, fiction is less generous than reality.

Ironically enough – but that is surely the danger of eradicating memory – Colin Monk feels that his own life is threatened by a nostalgia for the past that has resurfaced, totally reversing the old/new order: 'the deformed, the insane, the defective, the outcasts, the unhappy have become the new elite' (*IC* 342). 'Fair's fair' (*Ra* 138).

DAUGHTER BUFFALO – 'A TALE TOLD BY AN IDIOT'?

The title is as destabilizing as the whole novel. The reader is as bewildered as Daughter Buffalo itself: 'an expression of bewilderment exactly like her mother's' (*DB* 113); or as Turnlung after having had sex with Talbot (*DB* 145). The Pre-prologue on which it opens is a six-line poem by Turnlung which will be resumed later on. 'Turnlung's true home is the house of language, the city of words'.[17]

Turnlung is the old poet who is on the threshold of a death he announces in this prologue. He also hints at his slight madness, which might account for the strange tale he is telling us and which adds weight to the subtitle I have chosen. The whole novel hinges upon death – one of Frame's and the two characters' obsessions. Young Talbot is a doctor, who, after having studied embryology, now specializes in death. As at the beginning of *The Adaptable Man*, each of the two main characters introduces himself in turn with a very assertive 'I': 'I am Turnlung' (Prologue) and 'I am Talbot Edelman, medical graduate, a student of death' (*DB* 5).

Though Talbot seems to come from an ideal family, with a very domestic mother and an art-lover for a father (who always buys the same kind of picture), the first signs of its dysfunctioning, which may be representative of society at large, is the rejection of the grandfather whose existence Talbot discovers only when the old man is about to die. As in all her work, Frame denounces the strategies of avoidance around the taboos of death, old age, disease or 'imperfections' of all kinds which must be hidden from sight or relegated to the margins of a society that refuses to acknowledge them as part of life. The dead must be kept at 'a safe distance' or disposed of like garbage, on the 'rubbish dump'. The equation between the two is made explicit: 'Garbage may not be picked up; bodies may not be buried' (*DB* 31), or again: 'I may have been brought up in a world where both the animate and the inanimate are disposable' (*DB* 151). Ironically, despite his fascination with death, Talbot turns away from a man who is dying in the street, and will later reject Turnlung on account of his proximity to death (he lives near the funerarium). The dying man was too visible, obscenely so, if we are to believe Talbot: 'This death was a prolonged, persisting death [...] The man was groaning, trying to get his breath, lying in the middle of the sidewalk' (*DB* 80). And though he later tries to compensate for this unforgivable attitude towards a man who has been shot, he can barely hide his irritation at the mess the event has caused. It may be that Talbot can face death only when he can control it, as he does with his dog Sally on which he performs a number of operations and amputations that provoke her death, much to the indignation of Talbot's girlfriend, Lenore.

Lenore is a replica of Jenny – who is terrified of Alwyn's excesses – in *The Adaptable Man*. The two women's bodily perfection is their main source of attraction in their respective partners' eyes. Lenore's relation with Talbot had been founded on the shared experience of death: 'after death there seemed to be no other place to go except to love' (*DB* 18), a statement resumed at the end of the novel: 'the closest I have been to love has been my involvement with death' (*DB* 207). The intimate relation between death and love is illustrated in two concomitant episodes retold by Turnlung: 'two dogs began to copulate [...] they stayed together [...] What a strange afternoon of adhesiveness! [...] a linesman had been repairing the electric wires [...] he was held in a death lock' (*DB* 57–8). Love may be as fatal as death.

Talbot is another Frankenstein, dabbling in death: 'I learned to shop outside my home, in foreign lands, for some knowledge of myself and life and death, and to bring home like a hunter the twin trophies of creation and destruction' (*DB* 15). The fascination with death equals the wish to discover a secret, in which language alone can help: 'Language at least, may give up the secrets of life and death' (*DB* 29).

Turnlung's childhood story about the phonetic confusion between *dual* and *jewel* is revealing and very Frame-like. The Autobiography is filled with examples of lexical or phonetic discoveries, of the power of words, of the happiness but also of the betrayals they can lead to: 'Words, first words, are as traumatic as first love and first death' (*DB* 91–2). The *jewel* desks Turnlung had been dreaming of are merely *dual* desks. Some years later, he finds himself having to comment on the following poem: 'Death beauteous death, the jewel of the just' (*DB* 97). 'His childhood intimations of beauty (jewel-desks) which had been followed by disenchantment, loss of innocence and a greater awareness of the division of life (jewel/duel/dual), were finally recovered in a final apprehension of unity (death is the jewel, the original oneness)'.[18] There may lie the revelation of the secret.

The second part, entitled: 'The Bees in the Flowering Currant' gives an account of Turnlung's death-history, of 'all his dead ones', as if they were so many possessions (the reclaiming of Turnlung's body at the end echoes Tom Livingstone's in *Intensive Care*). His first human death, like Talbot's, was his grandfather's. When Talbot first meets him, he transforms him, but also himself, into his own grandfather, as if all three identities were fused and confused: 'Since Grandfather's death, I had become obsessed with elderly men in each of whom I saw the grandfather I never knew, who was hidden from me, whom I hid from myself [...] and I saw myself as an old man, I was face to face with myself' (*DB* 20). His very patronym – Edelman – is phonetically similar to the elder man he projects himself into. As Delbaere convincingly argues: 'In the total realm there are no separate identities; all forms, human and animal, animate and inanimate, are connected [...] death itself is a stage in creation – metamorphosis rather than extinction'.[19] In his death-history, Turnlung relates the story of an old friend of his and her two sisters' successive deaths in a highly autobiographical chapter on which the second part ends. In an unpublished article, Christine Favier draws the reader's attention to this unobtrusive change of narrators, one which has escaped critical notice. Chapter 9 is indeed no less than a piece of embedded autobiography. To parody Frame herself in one of her poems: 'Autobiography recurs' ('Sunday Drive'). Life ('bio') is never very far from one's writing ('graphy'). The one interpenetrates the other to the point that fiction and life are as inextricably linked as Frame herself believes and constantly illustrates. 'Reality seems to parody literature [...] The friend's narration functions like an embedded reflection of the two narrators' attitudes towards death'.[20] The friend, Janet-like, insists on the prestige death gives to a family, on the shower of clichés being poured upon them all, on the comfort provided by poetry (she quotes Shelley, Browning and Poe as Janet does in the Autobiography), but also on its pernicious role (as provider of clichés), on the tragic repetition of the first death with the second ill-named sister Joy, on the visit of the 'inhuman Lady Principal [who] could be broken down into human molecules' (*DB* 70). And as in the Autobiography, humour crops up in the midst of tragedy, as a form of self-defence and relief.

In the third part, 'Down, Instant Street, Jewels, and The Finishing Touch', Talbot and Turnlung meet again in the Natural History Museum before going to the zoo, two places where animals are either dead or imprisoned. The lion at the zoo looks almost dead: 'Its head appeared abnormally large in the small cage with the mane resembling a growth prompted by endocrine imbalance rather than by essential lionhood. The flesh on its hind legs hung loose like the shanks of an old man, and the testicles were dropped and withered, almost brushing the floor of the cage (*DB* 112).' After having offered him a room in his now empty flat (Lenore, his girlfriend, has left him), Talbot rejects Turnlung first by moving house to make sure he will not find him: 'I felt safe from Turnlung' (*DB* 149) and then by refusing to admit having ever met him when he goes to see his body at the morgue.

The epilogue is characteristic of Frame's usual endings: Turnlung has been in an old people's home for ages and the whole story we have been reading may be just a figment of his imagination, with Talbot just an invented character in a fictional work. His description of the landscape scene is a faithful replica of Talbot's picture in chapter 21. As in *Scented Gardens for the Blind*, as in *Living in the Maniototo*, or in *The Carpathians*, the reader has once more been manipulated. On their first meeting, Talbot asserts the veracity of Turnlung's existence: 'My God, I did not dream Turnlung' (*DB* 21). But Turnlung might have dreamed Talbot up. If, as Delrez argues, 'Talbot approaches Turnlung as a writer would his character' (*MU* 72), the reverse is just as true.

LIVING IN THE MANIOTOTO – 'THE FIGURE OF THE ARTIST AS (YOUNG) WOMEN'

Living in the Maniototo is probably Frame's work that best qualifies as post-modern fiction, 'in view of its readiness to exploit realism even as it tests the limits of realistic convention' (*MU* 75). Frame herself would certainly reject any 'labelling' as a restriction on the freedom of creativity, which Dell Panny's article successfully demonstrates. The main protagonist-narrator is multiselved: 'And I, Mavis Furness, Mavis Barwell, Mavis Halleton, [...] just Alice Thumb, or Ariella, Lokinia [...] Or Violet Pansy Proudlock, ventriloquist' (*LM* 11–12). As a writer, Mavis describes herself as 'part of the whole only, hypothenuse' (*LM* 68). Unlike many post-modernists, she is concerned with the 'wholeness' of the work of art. 'Hypothenuse' personifies 'the author'; the image holds good for Mavis as 'author' or Frame as author. The triangle is a model showing the connection between a writer and the work she creates.[21] Like the author herself, she has spent some time in a psychiatric hospital: 'I wrote, very quickly, my first book, *The Green Fuse*, where I described the years of my late teens which I spent in a psychiatric hospital, because at that time it was thought to be a crime, a sin, a sign of disease instead of dis-ease, to be suffering from unhappiness' (*LM* 27).

In *Faces in the Water*, Frame satirizes a society that considers mental illness as a sign of perversity, of 'childish naughtiness'. Mavis has buried two husbands, Lewis Barwell, 'drain-layer' and former medical student, the father of her two children, the man who never made it from 'septic tanks to high-class human plumbing' (*LM* 25), and Lance Halleton, a former French teacher turned obsessional debt-collector, who 'might have choked on a remembered idiom' (*LM* 64) as if his first job meant to have its revenge. Lance was as obsessed, too, with grammatical correctness as Janet herself (she regarded grammatical errors as mortal sins). Lance hunts down the arch-debtor, Yorkie Wynyard. He,

Mavis-like, borrows identities to avoid imprisonment and ends up being caught 'Masquerading as a debt-collector', Lance's replica or mirror image (*LM* 63). Though Mavis attends the aptly-named Howard Conway's writing classes, she eventually decides, Frame-like, to 'break the rules': 'because nothing in art is forbidden. By critics and teachers, yes. By the painters, writers, composers, sculptors, no' (*LM* 68). This is what *Living in the Maniototo* does indeed illustrate. To sum up Gina Mercer's analysis of the book, the 'multiselved' protean narrator/protagonist creates illusion, while showing that it is illusion. Mavis is a conjurer, a 'ventriloquist [...] an eavesdropper, a nothingness, a shadow, a replica of the imagined' (*LM* 12), every- or no-body: 'she is claiming to be any-woman or no-one in particular'.[22] And if Maniototo means 'plain of blood', it is also, as Dell Panny again convincingly argues, a paradigm.[23]

Dorothy Jones, for her part, sees the three locations where Mavis lives – Blenheim (New Zealand), Baltimore and Berkeley – as a reflection of Frame's post-colonial consciousness, as 'New Zealand, the key location in *Living in the Maniototo*, is defined [...] in relation to other countries'.[24] I agree with this analysis, although I would add that this also tallies with Frame's illustration of the phenomenon of replicas, which finds ample demonstration in the novel. New Zealand Blenheim is, like its twin city Baltimore, a place of violence: 'It's a violent suburb' (*LM* 21). Are the twin cities as mad as the lycanthropic twins Mavis remembers in relation to Adelaide, the Garretts' wolf-child, who died at 15, 'the antithesis of the Lamb of God'.[25] 'I still hear in my mind the sound of their barking, yelping, whimpering as they made their bizarre canine gestures to each other and in their adolescent awakenings tried to mate each other, like dogs' (*LM* 122–3), an echo to the 'wailing of the wind a sound like the howling of a wolf', in Baltimore (*LM* 29). 'Wolves in the city?' (*LM* 29), Mavis wonders. In Baltimore, the second place, Mavis visits her old friend Brian (who is probably a fictional John Money), who lives in a prison-like house: 'and began to work at the various locks on the outer and the inside doors, and after I'd manipulated the chain and its lock and was safe inside, I relocked the doors, replaced the chain and set the heavy iron bar in its two supports' (*LM* 30). Lonnie, the nephew from New Zealand who visits Brian, complains about the lack of outside (*LM* 100). He also is a physical replica of his usually tolerant uncle Brian (their hair and skin are similar) who surprisingly turns into 'the stern Victorian father-figure in response to Lonnie's theft of some silver dollars'.[26] The episode cannot but bring to mind the severe hiding Janet received from her just as severe father for having stolen just as little money.

Violence is also visited upon Tommy, Brian's artistic jeweller friend to whom Brian and Mavis pay a visit, and who is destroyed in front of their incredulous eyes by the magic powerful detergent Blue Fury, and quickly 'slipped out of our lives' (*LM* 40) as if (as in *Intensive Care*) nothing had happened. With this drastic unexpected death, Frame means to denounce the violence done to artists (Poe died miserably in Baltimore): 'Tommy, the artist, is ground down and overwhelmed by the destructive power of the dirty and violent city [...] Frame [...] is suggesting that advertising evokes a world quite inimical to the values artists must espouse'.[27] The world of advertising uses language as a tool to trick people, even destroy them. But this kind of 'new language' (*LM* 51) has nothing to do with Vera's primitive cry or Godfrey's ice-spelling. It usurps the place of true poetry, like Gerard Manley Hopkins's 'Glory be to God for dappled things' (*LM* 52), which Frame singles out as an influence on her own poetry. To Mavis, who reproached Lance with having given up his job as a French teacher, Lance answered: 'I've known more rape and murder and debt in language than there'll ever be in Blenheim. Suicide too!' (*LM* 59). This declaration tallies with Frame's own in an interview: 'Extreme words can play executioner'.[28] Mrs Tyndall, who works as a maid at Brian's, has been brainwashed by religious advertising 'sold' by Brother Coleman. Mavis, like Frame, is caught in this irreconcilable paradox: how can we denounce the treachery of language without at the same time using it ? That is what finds its expression in Mavis's indignant plea for language when she listens to Brother Cole: 'I have to cry out here that language is all we have for the delicacy and truth of telling, that words are the sole heroes and heroines of fiction. Their generosity and forgiveness make one weep' (*LM* 92).

The paradox of language finds its best illustration later, with the word 'guest' (once understood by young Janet as 'guess'): 'I still marvel at the idea of the 'guess towel', and at the richness of meaning within the words 'guest' and 'host' with a guest as originally a host, a stranger, hostis, an enemy' (*LM* 133). A word can mean both one thing and its opposite. It is dual (it is interesting that in French, the word 'hôte' means both 'guest' and 'host'). 'New Zealand was our host, the kind, *discriminating* host, and we were 'duty-bound' to be the respectful, grateful guests' (*LM* 151; italics mine) explains Zita later on. It is thanks to her book, *The Green Fuse*, that Mavis meets the Garretts who lend her their house in Berkeley when they go to Italy, where they accidentally die, leaving Mavis an improbable legacy, something which could happen 'only in "real life"' (*LM* 120). Among all the books she finds on the shelves, there is no Yeats, which prompts in Mavis an impulse to compensate for this lack by writing an anaphoric poem: 'A house without Yeats' (*LM* 114–15). The Garretts' house is full of replicas, as Irving and Trinity 'were keen on replicas' (*LM* 122), even replicas of replicas: 'I discovered that the house itself was full of likenesses, of replicas, prints of paintings, prints of prints, genuine originals and genuine imitation originals, imitation sculptures and twin original sculptures' (*LM* 17).

Hardly has Mavis settled in, when she receives a visit from two couples, Doris and Roger and Theo and Zita, who were friends with the Garretts. Theo is the handsome, narcissistic elderly man who had rescued Zita, Hungarian and forty years his junior, one of the 'happy few' who, like Godfrey in *The Rainbirds*, had qualified to emigrate to New Zealand, on account of hers and her family's perfection and adaptability: 'Everyone said you had to be extra clever and beautiful and good and healthy to get into New Zealand [...] Therefore it was only the quiet ones, like us, who were chosen, with all our arms and legs and cheerful smiles and clean hands and face and hair' (*LM* 147). In *Intensive Care*, Milly also desperately (and vainly) keeps on smiling to look as happy as one should. Zita's mother, though, never managed to fit in and remained silent, 'growing thin and old and grey' (*LM* 152) till she died. Some of the less adaptable people were taken to the 'plain of blood' (i.e. Maniototo) to be 'processed' (*LM* 151). The other couple, Doris and Roger, met in New Zealand before moving to London. Roger's dream is to make a solitary expedition to the desert for which he prepares by spending a few exhausting sweaty hours in a place called

'DESERT', on the edge of civilization which looks more like 'a stage setting or the location for a film or a dream' (*LM* 171–2) – just another replica? – and where he desperately expects a revelation that never comes. While they are waiting for him in a hotel room, Theo has a stroke which leaves him with a speech impediment. Mavis eventually decides to give him and Zita the house, though she insists on keeping the golden blanket for herself as a keepsake. The (un)expected return of the Garretts is just another of Frame's usual tricks, who, Mavis-like, has been playing with us from the beginning, blurring the boundaries between fiction and reality, making Mavis wonder, if, like the two couples, or maybe like all of us, she is not 'a replica of a replica dreaming of a replica of dreams' (*LM* 237), a character in fiction, as this self-reflexive novel tends to illustrate. On her return to Baltimore, Mavis hears of Brian/Brain's (*LM* 239) (we know the misprint is not intentional, but it could have been) death, the reality of which she questions. The very last sentence of the novel brings us back to the beginning, giving Mavis the last words: 'I, Violet Pansy Proudlock, Barwell, Halleton, Alice Thumb herself, would continue to live and work in the house of replicas, usefully, having all in mind – the original, the other, and the manifold' (*LM* 240). *Living in the Maniototo* might be said to resist interpretation, as if Frame were denying the 'unartistic' critics the pleasure of access to monolithic understanding: 'nothing in art is forbidden' (*LM* 68).

THE CARPATHIANS OR 'THE FLOWER OF MEMORY'

'The Carpathians are a great mountain system, extending from Bratislava to Orsovo, in crescent form... the region is wild and fertile and well wooded with oaks, beeches, evergreens, firs, and wild animals are found' (*Ca* 66).

The Carpathians is the last of Frame's novels, published after the Autobiography. But like all the rest of her fiction, it hinges upon the notions of memory, transmission and language. In the prologue, J.H.B. (whose full name – John Henry Brecon – we later discover) is the son of the main protagonist, Mattina, by Jake Brecon, her novelist husband. He has written a best-seller but has been suffering from writer's block for the past thirty years. We know from the beginning that what we are about to read has been written by John Henry, and the end should come as no surprise to us, since Mattina's death is already mentioned in the prologue.

The writing of John Henry's second novel has been triggered by two events: 'the rediscovery of the Memory Flower, and the discovery of what I have called the Gravity Star'.[29] The first part is entitled 'The Gravity Star'. Mattina, a rich American woman, decides to spend some time in Puamahara in New Zealand's North Island, to collect and record a stock of experiences that could feed her husband's imagination for a new novel, while satisfying her own curiosity: 'An urgency within her demanded that she 'know' how the rest of the world lived, how they felt, and behaved, what they said to one another, what they rejoiced in, despaired of, and dreamed about; and so, whenever she travelled, she sought the company of the 'natives', listened to their stories' (*Ca* 19). But Mattina's concern with factual detail links her to the kind of constricting realism that is at odds with imagination. Mattina is not unlike Mina Harker in *Dracula* (the link is suggested by the reference to *Dracula* (*Ca* 168)) in that she plays the role of amanuensis to her husband-novelist. Hers is what I would call a photographer's craving to capture reality and fix it, and it is just as ambiguous. Both Roland Barthes and Susan Sontag have emphasized the highly paradoxical status of photographs, which aim both at keeping people alive while simultaneously fixing them like dead butterflies in unescapable frames. Mattina's 'documentary mode'[30] extends to land, which, like a colonizer, she desperately wants to possess. She has bought land in the Bahamas, Hawaii, Portugal, Spain, and after the cataclysm in Kowhai Street, her first impulse is to buy the whole estate. Hene, the Maori woman who invites Mattina for a party on the marae, is percipiently aware of this general tendency to reify others, in visitors like her:

> We're distant enough from the rest of the world to be thought not to have feelings and lives of our own: both us and the Pakehas are at the long end of the poking stick – Look, *they* move, *they* speak, *they* walk, *they* think. Isn't it so, that the further away you are, the less you are known, the more easily you may lose your state of being human? For some of us, we've already lost it in our own land. (*Ca* 84; italics mine)

Puamahara is the land of the Memory Flower, but it has also become a dangerous, violent place (not unlike Baltimore in *Living in the Maniototo*) where old Madge is found murdered the day after Mattina's arrival. The culprit is an inmate of the Manuka Home, the institution for the mentally handicapped on the outskirts of the town. The James's daughter, Decima (a replica of mute Erlene in *Scented Gardens for the Blind*) who 'has no words' (*Ca* 106) lives there and sometimes visits her parents who, ironically enough, are piano tuners but are unable to decipher their daughter's silence. Ironically enough, too, she will be spared in the cataclysmic decimation of the whole street, thanks to the distant location of the institution. The sparing of Decima might be accounted for by the fact that she is one of Frame's fictional favourites.

We are introduced to the gallery of Kowhai Street's inhabitants: Hercus Millow, the man obsessed with the war, Ed Shannon the computer man whose wife hates the place, the Townsends with Rex's old mother, Connie. But the main figure there is the imposter novelist, Dinny Wheatstone, who gives her name to the title of the second part, and introduces herself as such. Dinny's manuscript, which she hands to Mattina, is in fact Mattina's own story, thus reinforcing the metafictional, embedded dimension of the whole novel. Dinny is the kind of poet/ prophet Mattina is not: 'the realistic thrust animating [Mattina's] quest finds a counterpart in the philosophy of imposterism defined by Dinny Wheatstone, Mattina's artist neighbour as an in-built capacity for 'disbelief in being, in self' (*Ca*. 51) which she considers an absolute pre-requisite to vision'.[31] Dinny is another Mavis, 'nothing and no-one' (*Ca* 51) or, like Mavis, every-thing and every-one.

It is in part III, entitled 'The Memory Flower', that the cataclysm takes place in the form of a midnight primitive clamour, followed by a deluge of letters that come to replace the old worn-out words. Frame stages a killing of language. All languages disappear and turn into dust in a deluge of graphemes: 'a pile of old letters of old alpahabets [...] that had lasted well, magnificently, but were now like the old god and goddesses who no longer could change or accept new growth and must perish to feed the birth of the new' (*Ca* 131). The disappearance of language, however, coïncides not with total annihilation, but with the promise of a new language and of a regenerated humanity in a new world. For society to stop functioning on exclusion and the fear of otherness, one must reintroduce in thought and language a multiple, proteiform dimension (as opposed to the old, dualistic manichean one).

This apocalyptic surrealistic event coincides with the disappearance of the noisy presence Mattina had been hearing in her bedroom, a reminder of the knocking on Malfred's door: 'there was a sound of breathing, as if an animal had been breathing rhythmically' (*Ca* 79). Delrez analyses this mysterious presence in terms of 'the living void of eclipsed reality',[32] otherwise embodied by both Decima and the Maoris, the marginalized 'others'. The cataclysm leaves the whole street empty and dead: 'Everyone in Kowhai street had died or been killed and removed. Except Mattina' (*Ca* 149).

Mattina is the sole survivor, entrusted with the task of remembering and recording. On her return home, where she is diagnosed as fatally ill (exactly as Dinny, the visionary, had predicted), she tells her story to Jake and makes him promise to go to Puamahara. *The Carpathians* is a story of transmission, a plea against oblivion, the oblivion of those who, like Hene's people or the Decimas of this world, have been relegated to the margins of society. Mattina's expedition has been an initiation into the necessity of memory : 'She survives, though mortally ill, faced with the task of getting her story out through these fictive layers (reality boxes?) to husband Jake, who will tell it to son John Henry, who has written it as fiction, read by us reading Janet Frame's 11th novel'.[33]

The last part, entitled 'Housekeepers of Ancient Springtime', which had been suggested as the original title of the novel,[34] stages Jake's pilgrimage to Puahamara where he meets old Connie, another of the survivors, the memory of the town, who just confirms that 'the whole street disappeared' (*Ca* 184): 'I am the only one now who remembers, the only one left' (*Ca* 184). Jake's visit to Decima is the last homage paid to the forgotten ones. Jake in turn vows to tell John Henry (who is the writer he himself has never been, as he has actually managed to write a second book) the story we have just been reading. John Henry's book is the fulfillment of his two parents' will (in the two meanings of the term). Memory will not die, but flower.

4

Short Stories and Poems: Generic Variety

THE SHORT STORIES: *THE LAGOON, YOU ARE NOW ENTERING THE HUMAN HEART* **AND** *THE RESERVOIR*

> It is little wonder that I value writing as a way of life when it actually saved my life. (II 106)

The first collection of short stories, *The Lagoon*, introduces the reader to nearly all the subjects with which Frame will concern herself in her later fiction: the lives of children, the lives of the 'mad', the lives of the solitary, the unsuccessful, the inadequate, the marginals and those whose cry for 'Help' is repeated throughout the novels. In 'My Last Story', the narrator first says: 'I'm never going to write another story' (*La* 110) and ends with these words: 'I think I must be frozen inside with no heart to speak of. I think I've got the *wrong* way of looking at Life' (*La* 112; italics mine). With *The Lagoon*, Frame won the Hubert Church Award and was spared the lobotomy she was about to undergo a few days later. 'Writer Wins Prize for Prose': 'The New Zealand centre of [...] PEN announces that the Hubert Church Memorial award for prose has been won by Miss Janet Frame of Oamaru for her book "Lagoon and other stories" (*WA* 112). In the Autobiography, the announcement is made by the doctor: "You've won the Hubert Church Award for the best prose. Your book, *The Lagoon*.' I knew nothing about the Hubert Church Award. Winning it was obviously something to be pleased about. I smiled. 'Have I?' 'Yes. And we're moving you out of this ward. And no leucotomy." (II 108) This crucial episode is related almost verbatim in Jane Frame's novel *Faces in the Water*.

You Are Now Entering The Human Heart is composed of twenty-five stories of unequal length ('Snowman Snowman', written twenty years before the publication of the collection, covers seventy pages) that span fourty years of Frame's life. Seven of the short stories in *The Reservoir*, published twenty years before, are resumed in the later collection, and the thirteen others read like variations on the Autobiography or some of the other stories. All of them are interwoven with autobiographical details; the trips overseas (in 'Burial in Sand'), 'Royal Icing' on Christmas cakes, anticipate the 'words and phrases that could be eaten' (I 96), etc. Frame takes fact as raw material for her fiction, with a view to illustrating her creed: 'Reality, the ore of the polished fiction' (III 19). 'Keel and Kool' is structured around the sister's death, and so, too, is 'The Stink-Pot' in *The Reservoir*, where the sister (Molly), conflates the real Myrtle of the Autobiography with the fictional Joan of 'Keel and Kool'. Both Molly and Joan are called 'liars' by the jealous suffering narrators. The title is repeated at the very end of the story, underlining its key function in the text. 'The Bull Calf' evokes Janet's love for their two cows, Scrapers and Bluey, 'who' are also in the poems and in *Towards Another Summer*, etc. Frame's favourite themes are all there: childhood ('My Cousins – Who Could Eat Cooked Turnips', 'Swans'), the power of imagination, solitude ('The Terrible Screaming', 'The Teacup', 'The Bath', 'The Day of the Sheep'), all linked to the difficulties of interpersonal communication and the inadequacies of language.

Throughout the stories, Frame emphasizes the importance of ordinary things, events or situations whose apparent insignificance is transformed by the alchemy of writing in a very restricted space. By definition, the short story is short and, like a picture, it concentrates on a single effect, on a particular experience in a self-contained world, where everything (titles, endings, onomastics, toponymy) carries significance. Frame's prose, here as in all her fiction, is poetic, allying scrupulous realism with dream and fable. My analysis of the short stories is organized around the theme of difference, presented in all its variety, but always perceptible through language and the use that the different characters make of it. Adults and children are opposed in the way they speak (whereas the language of children is simple and straightforward, adults resort to clichés and euphemisms to 'beat about the truth'). This dichotomy is reproduced on a larger scale in a society that rejects and condemns whatever fails to 'follow the rules'. The consequences are dire; solitude and death are the lot of those who cannot or will not conform. This is not to say that there is no perspective at all. As throughout her work, Frame proposes a solution through language in a renewed form, in an enterprise of deconstruction that will lead to a successful reconstruction.

In 'Keel and Kool', Frame chooses a particular day (a family picnic with a friend, as in the Autobiography) in Winnie's life. Winnie is a third-person narrator whose elder sister Eva (a fictional Myrtle) has just died. Eva's death is the pivotal event in the short story, dictating the behaviours of the adults and of the two girls. Frame's favourite themes are all present: family, death, childhood, nature. The mother tries to forget Eva's death by reading a magazine, whereas the father, after taking a photograph (the French word is also 'cliché') of 'a happy family' (*La* 18) goes fishing, bent double under the weight of fate. 'Frame draws attention to the cultural convention, the verbal equivalent of the ellipsis, of avoidance and pretence, especially in regard to death' (*SF* 24). Winnie (the narrator) plays with Joan, but the game quickly turns into a struggle for the possession of Eva. Winnie knows she has lost, but tries to keep up appearances by fighting back and pushing Eva over. The link between the world of fantasy and reality is established through the story of the albatross and Joan as a kind of siren/witch with green hair. 'Winnie revisits fairy-tales, legends (the Homeric siren) and romantic poetry. The Albatross makes its appearance as 'a Christian soul/ We hailed it in God's name' and we must not kill.[1] Her rebellion, however, is only short-lived and Winnie has to cope with her suffering alone, fearing a future without Eva as well as a rejection from her family because of her behaviour towards Joan. The last sentence – 'And Kool would never come, ever' (*La* 25) – of the story resumes the title while enhancing its prevailing pessimism and nostalgia. Bird-like up in her tree, Winnie desperately calls for Kool, who remains mute. The attempt to recreate the lost nest of sisterly union is a failure. The children are not 'such happy little things' (*La* 19) as the mother (a champion in the art of clichés) would like to think (a proleptic echo to what she will say about Janet when she is in a psychiatric ward). She refuses to use the very word 'death' replacing it with euphemisms such as 'passed' or 'gone' and relying on the deceiving trick of photos ('you've got her photo, it's always nice to have their photos' (*La* 20)) to make herself believe they will compensate for her loss. This is also because people have to look happy ('a happy family'), to conform at all costs, and not to betray any weakness.

Another example of the power of taboo (this time in the field of sex) is 'The Bullcalf'.[2] Olive, another fictionalized double of Janet (a faithful replica of young Janet Frame herself with whom nobody wanted to form twos at school) does not understand why the bull is bleeding and her parents, smiling knowingly, refuse to tell her the truth because sex, or anything related to it, or to the body (human or animal – in fact the bull has been castrated) is taboo. The child is out of the world (and words) of adults. That is also the case in 'The Reservoir' or 'Obstacles' (*Re*), where the children try to imitate adult practices whilst all the time laughing at them. The episode is resumed in *Towards Another Summer*. Children are more like the spectators of an adult game, however paradoxical that may sound, because adults are playing at being 'within', whereas children or 'marginal' adults remain excluded.

In 'My Cousins – Who Could Eat Cooked Turnips', the narrator stages two groups of children. On the one hand, there are those who can and want to eat the vegetable and, on the other, the rest (including the narrator) who refuse because, for them, cooked turnips are the worst thing to eat imaginable. The first group is the epitome of conformism and obedience: they eat the turnips because they are told to. What is at stake here is obviously not the turnips but the broader attitude to life. The narrator despises her too-obedient 'turnip-eating' cousins, refusing to individualize them (they are just 'my cousins', with no first names) before the more optimistic ending where a form of harmonious communication is reached through mutual tolerance for 'the other', however different that person may be.

Frame's fiction is inspired by her own life, a perpetual struggle between individual desires and the demands of a strict society abiding by Victorian principles and condemning any step aside. To feel and to be integrated into the world around, means conforming to it at the risk of letting go of one's identity, sublimating one's desires, not to say oneself. To be excluded, either voluntarily or at the behest of a society which ostracizes someone on the grounds of difference (and Frame herself knows what this means), offers little if any, by way of solution, to the individual in question. Is there any possible reconciliation between the individual's desires and the demands of society? To be included, within the society in which one lives, means to conform to the rules. Conformism means comfort. Being normal means respecting the norm. In 'The Teacup', the two women know that being single (like Malfred, Zoe or the Miss Abson of 'An incident in mid-ocean' in *The Reservoir*) could mean being singled out, different, marginal. Hence the desperate need to find a husband, especially as they get old. Edith goes so far as to try and ensnare one, by every means in her power, inviting Bill to share her flat, offering him a teacup, doing everything she can to keep him, to the point that he can bear it no longer and leaves without a word. Her efforts are counterproductive. The text is an inverted fairy-tale with Joycian overtones since Edith is a sort of desperate Eveline, the eponymous heroine of Joyce's short story. Ted in 'The Advocate' (that comes just after 'The Teacup' in the collection) also (over)does his best to please people, to make them (and himself) believe everyone loves him, though he knows that it is all pretence and sham. Once he has been 'unmasked', he can bear it no more and commits suicide, leaving the spiteful people who had mocked him, hypocritically praising him for his numerous qualities now that he is dead ('Over his dead body' (*HH* 172)) because this is what happens when people die, whatever their lives might actually have been like. Frame denounces the power of clichés, especially in the field of illness, death and sex.

The elderly lady in 'The Bath' is neglected, not to say completely forgotten, simply because she is old and useless like the rejected objects the children find on the rubbish dump in *Owls Do Cry*. It is better to be young, rich and happy, which is what Ted had been trying to be to the point of dying for it, instead of telling the truth about his utter loneliness. Loneliness is but another form of weakness. Everybody should have friends, go out, enjoy life, spend money, smile. In *Intensive Care*, Milly does her best to look happy in the hope she might avoid being destroyed. Ted is an emblematic figure. He appears as a social success, on a human, social and professional level (the accumulative style is the expression of all the forms of his successes), for which the reader himself is summoned as witness. The invasive repetition of Ted's name accentuates his omnipresence. In the street, at work, in his family, Ted is needed and useful. No one can do without him. He is full of good intentions, generous, friendly, respectful of the law. He is 'over-integrated' as the intensives, the qualifiers and the exclamations ironically testify. The text is built on two clearly opposed parts, the first listing his successes in all fields (but *he* is the only narrator and his reliability is questionable) and the second exposing the reality of a life that has nothing to do with the previous idyllic description. Ted's life is so fake that it leads to his suicidal death. Through him, Frame denounces the social conformism that forces its people to adopt an ethic of success whose sterility ends in death. Ted dies for a life that has been nothing but a lie. The conclusion at this point is the reiteration of the sentence 'he has many friends', or: he is 'the man with many friends', the phrase sounding like a qualifier, a label. The following part is structured around the key word 'alone', an obsessive theme in Frame's writings. And it sheds a retrospective light on the earlier part, denouncing Ted's life as a complete illusion and self-delusion.

Society is 'they', the paranoid pronoun that permits to share the guilt around: 'anonymity drapes a kind of emotional velvet' (*IC* 228) over the evolving tragedy. The only solution for Ted is to choose death as an evasion, a way not to be found out. His death also sets him apart from ordinary folk. He has committed suicide and that excludes him from authorized burial ground. Even in death, he is isolated and finds no compassion. His is 'a suicide' (*HH* 172), with the word referring both to the act and to him (an echo to the eponymous poem, 'The Suicides' (*PM* 72)) as if death deprived him of his identity. The narrator's judgement seems to confirm that Ted's choice, given his situation, was the only solution. In the end, the story seeks to denounce the world's manicheism. Things should not be so clear-cut. There is no right or wrong way of behaving and it is only because Ted thought that there was that he loses his life. Ted could be anyone and his life could be anybody's. Frame's concerns are all there: society and the individual, solitude and death. Ted's obstinate efforts cost him his life. Conformism, carried to excess, is the death of the individual. In *Owls Do Cry*, Chicks meets with a similar fate.

As in *Living in the Maniototo*, Frame denounces consumerism and materialism. Adverts (in 'The Bull Calf') play a crucial part, stressing the need to be like everybody else. Society aims at uniformity, at erasing difference. To sum up the French feminist critic Hélène Cixous's theory: 'The paradox of otherness is that, of course, at no moment in History is it tolerated or possible as such. The other is there only to be reappropriated, recaptured, destroyed as other.[3]

That is what happened to Frame herself, with dramatic consequences. Frame denounces the behaviour of those adults who have appropriated the demands of society, to the point of making them theirs and believing that they are the only possible way of life. That is why she often chooses children as narrators because theirs is a more natural and less constrained point of view and it is easier for them to denounce the attitudes of conformist adults.

In 'The Day of the Sheep', the sheep stands for Nance and her boring, miserable life, which is the lot of many people. Mercer sees Nance as a double of Chicks, who are both no more than stray sheep. Frame resorts to the device of choosing animals as the characters in her stories (for example 'The Two Sheep'), all the more so as sheep are known for their docility and gregariousness, hence the surprise at finding a stray sheep in a washhouse, as if the sheep had escaped its fate, as Nance and Tom would like to do ('We'll go away from here' (*La* 47)). They dream of somewhere else, like the mother in 'The Pictures', searching in the films she sees for a kind of 'artificial paradise', away from the awful, solitary boarding house where she lives. The woman lives alone with her little girl, another form of difference that accounts for her sadness (a recurrent theme throughout the text), which links her to the old woman in 'The Bath', who finds comfort only in her visits to the churchyard and in the thought that she will soon join her husband, thus resuming a 'normal' way of life, ironically enough, in death. The old woman can barely move, she is almost handicapped, and society values health to the point of considering illness a sin (as the narrator puts it in *Faces in the Water*) whereas the children value difference as a form of prestigious aura: longing to be struck with 'Infantile paralysis' (*HH* 134), an illustration of what Frame's mother wanted her children to believe, equating illness with genius.

If the topics Frame deals with are often tragic, her way of dealing with them is often comic. Humour is not only rhetorical, it is also philosophical, an attitude of looking at life, from a healthy distance. However, the most striking feature of Frame's writing is her way of experimenting with language, playing on words, and literalizing metaphors. In 'Solutions', the narrator/character wants to become a mere spirit. To achieve his aim, he gradually excises parts of his body that he considers cumbersome, an obstacle on the way to the elevation of the mind. He wants to be rid of his body completely and ends up as a dried-up prune, which the three little mice eat for breakfast. As in *Mona Minim and the Smell of the Sun*, the fairy-tale is deconstructed from the start as the well-known incipit of fairy-tales is parodied into: 'It happened once – twice, thrice? – upon a time' (*HH* 113), a hint that this is not going to be a 'normal' fairy-tale. Frame is a word-taster whose poetic use of language allows her to transform reality, to make comic what is not, to make the insignificant significant as if she were a magician with a pen for a wand.

Her humour sometimes verges on irony or satire, especially when she attacks the taboo of death, as in 'The Mythmaker's Office' that stages a dystopian, 1984-like dictatorship where it is forbidden to die. The story is the account of an absurd decree forbidding people to die, or even pronounce the word 'death'. This story reads like a remake of *1984* by George Orwell, a dictatorial society forbidding its members to do natural things (such as making love in *1984*). Of course, the society she depicts is a caricature, but that may be the best way she has found to denounce the excesses to which conformism can lead. The solution lies in avoiding the fatal word altogether, as if avoidance or silence could be performative: not saying the word might make death disappear. 'Don't say that word, kiddies' (I 107), the mother used to tell the children about the morgue. The word 'Death' is capitalized, as if it were the arch-enemy. The dead, like the mad, the old, the poor, are 'relegated to the outskirts of the city', to become invisible (the invisibility of death is also the main topic of 'Snowman, Snowman'). Hospitals become 'unmentionable', and even doctors are banned because of their link with death. They have become politically incorrect. But repression is so depressing that the avoidance of death ironically leads to suicide. In the second part of the story, we witness an invasion of death, that touches everything and everyone, as if it were taking its revenge after long years of repression and prohibition. Only one couple survives, a parody of Adam and Eve in a Paradise turned Hell, where the sun is 'invalid [...] erupting its contagious boils of light' (*HH* 111) (which may be an allusion to the Plague, also called the Black Death).

Language itself becomes contaminated. 'Let's make Death' (*HH* 111) is an obvious parody of the more usual: 'Let's make peace/love'. So, from a constant wish to experiment with language, Frame poeticizes reality, but also (and more deeply), denounces the taboos rooted in society, by pinpointing their absurdity. Her subversion may be only literary, but it is nonetheless very powerful. She aims to recover the aborted or unexplored potential of words, just as she does with the first volume of the Autobiography, and its distorted pronounciation: 'Is-Land', once more refusing (against Myrtle's advice), to silence the mute 's', which has as much right to exist as the other letters. For Frame, the only exit is through language.

Frame's tone in the short stories is ironical and even satirical. She presents society as the villain against which the individual must fight if he is not to be devoured by it. The example of Ted is revealing. His make-believe costs him his life. In 'The Terrible Screaming' the stranger (this is an alternative narrative persona), dares not say he has heard the scream for fear of being thought mad (once again, this has strong autobiographical echoes). He is actually admitted to a rest home (the euphemistic name for a psychiatric asylum, a proleptic echo to the narration of Frame's own internment in the Autobiography). The stay in psychiatric hospitals is also the subject of 'The Bedjacket', 'Snap-Dragons' and 'The Park': is there a way out of it? 'The Terrible Screaming' ends on an intensely ironic paradox: 'Silence had found its voice' (*HH* 197). Silence might also be a refuge, or a place of resistance (as illustrated in *Scented Gardens for the Blind* through the character of Erlene/Vera). But Frame also denounces the refusal to speak out, to say what one feels for fear of disturbing the prevailing order, the recourse to 'strategies of avoidance' such as clichés, euphemisms, 'ways of not saying things as they are' (beating about the bush, the words, the truth). The word 'illusion' (*HH* 107) is a key signifier in the story. Ted also lives in a world of illusions. The Snowman in the eponymous story has the (very human) illusion that he is immortal, just as people have the illusion they are happy.

'Snowman Snowman' has a special status, since it is the longest of all the stories. But it is also concerned with life and death. The point of view is that of a snowman who comments on the lives of human beings and on his own, which is altogether more fragile, but also superior to human beings. He engages in conversation with Perpetual Snowflake 'a voluble spirit stationed on the Dincer family's windowsill whose *raison d'être* is to assist the Snowman in his predicament and to guide him in life towards some sort of ontological and epistemological breakthrough'.[4] The nine-part story opens with the birth/fabrication (by Rosemary Dincey) of Snowman and ends with his death. At first sight, the story could be another fairy-tale, but it is more akin to an allegory interspersed with fragments of life stories. Rosemary is run over by a lorry, and her death is but another opportunity for the narrator to denounce the taboo of death. Her body must be removed since it might frighten the living (as mental illness does). Death should remain hidden. Not unlike human beings, Snowman desperately wants to believe in his immortality and is enlightened only at the cost of decomposition. The story oscillates between realism, poetry and the marvellous, with philosophical and metaphysical overtones in a truly Framean style.

In short, Frame's is a pessimistic view of life but her tone is often humorous, even if it does not aim at concealing the pathetic inefficacy of conformism carried to excess. By dint of trying to adapt, to conform, to be 'within', the individual can suffocate, even die (as is the case with Ted). 'Temporary masks, I knew, had their place; everyone was wearing them, they were the human rage; but not masks cemented in place until the wearer could not breathe and was eventually suffocated' (II 63). Frame reinscribes taboo subjects in her writing, showing that one can create a 'world of one's own', with 'a language of one's own' not necessarily through any open rebellion, but through words, in the power of which she has always believed.

POEMS – *THE POCKET MIRROR, THE GOOSE BATH*

'I wanted to be a poet' is Janet Frame's firm declaration reproduced in the Autobiography (I 114) and *Towards Another Summer* (*TAS* 188). As an unconditional worshipper of Imagination, she saw poetry as the best medium to express it. In an interview she declared: 'Poetry is the highest form of literature because you can have no dead wood in a poem'.[5] As a child, she wrote a poem for school: 'When the sun goes down and the night draws nigh/ and the evening shadows touch the sky [...]' (I 83). Myrtle wanted her to substitute 'touch' for the more poetic 'tint': 'At home that evening, the writing of that first poem sparkled my first argument over writing as an art' (I 83).

Though Janet seems to comply with her sister's wishes, in deference to her age and superior knowledge, she nonetheless reverts to her original choice when she later writes the poem in her notebook. Janet's rebellion is textual. This significant anecdote illustrates her (early) choices, her subversion of the existing codes, be it in her fiction, her prose or poetry. She means to have it her 'own way'. This is how she puts it after the discussion with Myrtle: if there are 'words and phrases you [had] to use' (I 83), she refuses them and replaces them with 'words of her own', not unlike Milly Galbraith in *Intensive Care*, whose phonetic spelling gives access to the inner truth, to the 'lining of words' (*Ra*), as does Janet's famous 'Is-Land' where the 'S' is extracted from an unjustified silence. Poetic conventions are a brake on the imagination, though Janet sometimes yields to their power, resorting to childish performative/magic strategies:

> I wrote a poem about dreams, believing that if I used the word
>   *dream* repeatedly, in some way I would be creating dreams:
> I dream of misty hills at dawn
> I dream of skies when it's morn
> How could anyone, reading those lines, deny I was a dreamer?
>
>   (I 115); (JF's italics)

In *The Pocket Mirror*, one short poem is entitled 'Dream', but the very word has disappeared from the text, as if she had now proved that she was at last the dreamer she had so often dreamed of becoming.

However, her poetry has received far less critical attention than the rest of her production. As Valérie Baisnée says in her chapter 'A Home in Language: The (meta)physical World of Janet Frame's Poetry',[6] she did not even take herself seriously as a poet. And she 'was wretchedly conscious that [she] had none of the disability esteemed in poets' (I 116). With her usual sense of humour, which has perhaps been insufficiently noticed and praised, Frame declared: 'Poetry is my first love. I unfortunately don't feel that I've ever been able to write a real poem, but I keep trying' (GB 12). She has indeed been trying a lot.

The Pocket Mirror is the title of the whole collection and also of one of the poems (*PM* 62). There are altogether 168 poems in *The Pocket Mirror* and a further 123 in *The Goose Bath*, which was published posthumously following an order and a division into seven sections chosen by her niece, Pamela Gordon (Foreword), Denis Harold (Afterword) and Bill Manhire (Introduction).

If most of her poems are included in the two above-quoted volumes, her poetic production far exceeds them, which makes it impossible to deal with the whole of her output. Many poems appeared in newpapers and reviews, such as *Landfall*. In *Wrestling With The Angel*, Michael King relates the autobiographical episode in which Frame had published a few poems, pretending she was West Indian. They were returned because the language 'did not quite come up to the standard of English required' (*WA* 150). Frame herself concluded: 'In a sense my literary lie was an escape from a national lie that left a colonial New Zealander overseas without any real identity' (III 29). In the explanatory notes to *The Goose Bath*, the authors draw our attention to the links between Frame's poetry and prose: many poems have 'prose versions', such as 'The Servant', 'The Worms' (related in both the Autobiography and *Towards Another Summer*). 'The Specimen in the Maudsley Brain Museum' differs slightly from the one printed in chapter 15 of *The Envoy From Mirror City* (*GB* 208). Baltimore is one of the three 'B' cities in *Living in the Maniototo*. Bill, her cousin who shot his lover, her parents and himself (*WA* 287) is fictionalized in *Intensive Care* and 'poeticized' by Frame in 'Big Bill' (*PM* 5). Frame herself refers to this mutability, which once again illustrates her creed in the fluidity of the boundaries between the different genres, or between life and writing: 'I have always thought there was something magical about writing, and how it can be changed, buried, resurrected, influenced, and even added to by others with their own point of view. Very often a poem becomes a novel' (*GB* 202). In her fiction, the characters who are 'different' speak in poetic prose, such as Daphne's italicized monologues in *Owls Do Cry*, or Naomi's in *Intensive Care*. Daphne's prose is 'at times completely paired down to poetry'.[7] It is perhaps no more different for Frame to write poetry or prose than to write fiction or autobiography. As Valérie Baisnée shows, the novels and the Autobiography are interspersed with poems, be they Frame's own invention or quotations from famous poets, such as Shelley, Yeats, Auden or others. We can sometimes even wonder who the author really is, as Frame, in her Frame-like way, never stops playing with her readers and never intends to give them the answer. 'Literary quotations, poems inserted within a narrative, and folk-rhymes create an intertextual web of cultural references that run throughout her work and act as original viewpoints on her fiction. In the novel *Intensive Care*, poems are like a Greek chorus that link the various strands of the story.'[8]

The poems span a great variety of topics, and some are recurrent, almost as obsessive as they are in her fiction. In 'The Suicides' (*PM* 72), Frame tries to empathize with 'the kind of despair they must have known', whereas in 'Another Country' (*PM* 98), she sympathizes with the 'undertakers [who] do not choose to undertake [to] grow the tree that provides the wood for the coffin of man woman and child'. In *The Goose Bath*, 'The Dead' (and its Joycian title) 'have worn out my grief' (*GB* 186). In one of the last poems, 'What I have seen or dreamed' (*GB* 193), her concluding line sums it all up: 'the principal thing seen and dreamed is Death', with its eloquent capital D. As in the Autobiography, where Frame declared she was more at ease with animals than with human beings, Nature is omnipresent in 'Season' (*PM* 12) and 'the Tree' (*PM* 25). It is 'going to be cut down any day' (line 1), as it was in *Intensive Care*. In her chapter on the poems, Valérie Baisnée emphasizes the importance and significance of trees in the poems: 'Images of trees are at the center of Frame's landscape awareness [...] Trees are a major source of metaphors, and provide a structural link between poems'[9]; but so do animals, especially birds ('Birds are on the wing everywhere', *GB* 21) and cats ('The Golden Cat', *PM* 69;

'The Cat of Habit', *GB* 177 and 'The Tom Cat Which Sargeson Refused to Have Neutered', *GB* 45), but also, beetles ('Sunday Drive') or, quite unexpectedly, fleas (*GB* 75), in a poem which is as short as fleas are small:

> Fleas are fleas
> because they do as they please

As for foxes (the last poem of *The Pocket Mirror*) and cows, they were the companions of her childhood. In the poem entitled 'For Paul on His Birthday' (*GB* 36), Frame evokes their common 'railway' childhood. An accompanying note explains that 'this poem is addressed to [her] friend Paul Wonner [...] The first line is an allusion to Edith Nesbit's classic children's novel *The Railway Children* (1906). The quotation ('Reste Tranquille si soudain l'Ange à ta table se décide') is from the sequence *Vergers* (Orchards), written in French by the German poet Rainer Maria Rilke' (*GB* 207), and this is also the epigraph to the second volume of the Autobiography. In 'Sunday Drive' (*PM* 14), which is written in dialogic form, the child declares that her favourite toy is 'a kerosene tin', an echo to her famous 'God Save our Gracious *Tin*' (I 15; author's italics) in the Autobiography and *Towards Another Summer*. Frame's love of words is nowhere more blatant than in the poems. One poem is actually entitled 'Words' (*PM* 42) and opens on a quotation from Auden: 'Words are for those with promises to keep'.

As they vary in topics, the poems also vary in form and length: some read almost like limericks, or nursery rhymes, some are nonsensical, like 'Lament For The Lakes' (*PM* 70): 'the colback talkus' or 'Last Will And Testament' (*PM* 78), 'When collade wolders fail'. '*The Pocket Mirror* is characterized by a great variety of forms: haiku-type poems alternate with long poems bordering on other genres of discourses, such as letters, narratives or dialogues [...] Frame also stages her aesthetic conflicts in scenarios ranging from the comical to the tragic'.[10] 'The Fahrenheit Man' belongs to the first:

> The fahrenheit man
> on the centigrade sea
> with wittage and wantage
> and wastage and me

(*PM* 79)

Frame plays with sounds, words and alliterations, which she also does in her poems concerned with war and mass destruction (two recurrent themes in *Intensive Care*). 'Napalm' is one of them: the alliterations and assonances together with the disposition of the words on the page 'make fire with less than two vowels rubbed together' (*PM* 66).[11] 'Instructions for Bombing with Napalm' (*PM* 18) reads like a frightful recipe: 'concoct ointment/ultimate oil/unction/lotion/count coil'. An exploding bomb is also the topic of the poem 'People are ill, dying' (*PM* 45).

Frame recognized the influence of such poets as Shelley, Keats, Wordsworth, Rilke, Dylan Thomas, Gerard Manley Hopkins, George Barker (to quote but a few), by quoting them directly or alluding to them obliquely. In 'The Cat Has a Mouthful of Larks', we read: 'Shelley himself would be forced to practice economy/both of skylark and of simile' (*GB* 164). When she was in London, near Hampstead Heath, she quoted Keats's 'La Belle Dame sans Merci' to herself (*WA* 150).

As she realized after her sisters' successive deaths, poetry brings comfort to the bereaved, who discover their own sufferings in the words of others. This is expressed in the following lines from 'Annabel Lee': 'It was many and many a year ago/In a kingdom by the sea' (I 111–12). Poetry arouses welcome feelings of recognition and gratitude (it is interesting that the French word 'reconnaissance' is the same for both), as when she has the epiphany at Ibiza with the discovery of 'tumbleweed'. In Ibiza, the feeling of familiarity away from home is triggered by words. The first poem in *The Pocket Mirror* is entitled 'Dunedin Poem' and the last is dedicated to Wyndham, the other place that 'has stayed secure in its mutinous dream' (*PM* 120). The sense of place is acute in Frame's work, as in many post-colonial writers' works, but maybe even more so in her case, where it is both his/torical and 'her/storical' "Where is 'my place' in the world?' is the question that runs throughout Frame's poetry and Autobiography'.[12] As an adolescent she felt a terrible 'homelessness of self' (I 136), to the point that the psychiatric hospital became a welcome refuge. The experience in hospital is the subject of the poem 'Flo' (*PM* 59): 'she died you know where/in a back ward mad' and also of 'Hospital Dance' (*GB* 41). As she writes in 'Sunday Drive':

'Memory recurs, cripples. There is no relief from its pain' ('Sunday Drive', *PM* 15). The refuge is also a trap: there is no escaping the unforgettable, in spite of the nurse's advice in *Faces in the Water*.

Poetry, however, may play the redemptive role in a world heading for its own destruction. That is what Frame tries to do in her fiction, which is altogether aesthetic and political. Valérie Baisnée demonstrates that *poetry* is different from *poem*, in so far as the first is inscribed in a tradition whereas the second is a personal act. This tallies with Terry Sturm's distinction between 'langue and parole': Frame wants to speak with her own words, to fight against the comfortable, worn-out clichés, even if, as Baisnée perciplently argues, she has greater affinity with her contemporaries than she is prepared to admit: 'Frame is haunted by *doxa*, by the fear of repeating something already said and already thought. This is very much a contemporary obsession [...] Thus, in her aversion to convention, Frame is, ironically, closer to her contemporaries than she thinks' (italics, Baisnée's).[13] Frame (but she is not the only one) is always caught in this double-bind: how can one express oneself outside language when language is one's means of expression? 'She is [...] defined solely by the words and the associations she creates, and, in delivering language from the traditional images inherited from the code, [...] she hopes to offer a better vision of the real world.'[14]

MONA MINIM AND THE SMELL OF THE SUN

Janet Frame said that this book for children was her favourite. Whether we are willing to suspend our disbelief when we read it, or not, does not really matter. Here, as in *Scented Gardens for the Blind*, where the blackbeetle plays a key part, insects again 'people' her fiction. *Mona Minim* has not received much critical attention, apart from Marc Delrez's recent article entitled 'The legacy of invention: Determinism and metafiction in Janet Frame's *Mona Minim and The Smell of the Sun*'.[15] Mona is a young House Ant (as opposed to the Garden Ants) who lives a happy life at home, among her family and with her best friend Pamela (the name of Frame's niece) but who leaves the nest one day, in quest of adventure and independence. Not unlike Lewis Carroll's Alice, she falls down a crack in the stairs, but is saved by Barbara, a young Garden Ant who introduces her into her community where she spends most of her adult life before returning home to rescue Barbara who has been made a prisoner in the Ant Farm.

The tale is articulated around three movements that correspond to three periods in Mona's life: childhood (most of Frame's stories are concerned with childhood), which she spends at home; adolescence and early adult age at the 'other' place; and finally maturity and old age back home. That could be called 'the three ages of Mona' and it is no less than the story of a life. Mona's patronym hints at her size – she is dimininutive – her youth and her inexperience, which she constantly uses as pretexts to procrastinate or avoid doing what is expected of her.

The story starts like a traditional fairy-tale: 'Once upon a time', but is immediately corrected with the addition: 'not long ago, almost now' (*MM* 1). As in the short story 'Solutions', Frame rewrites the fairy-tale motif, not only in form but also in content: 'she delineates a fictional universe which gives uncomfortable centrality to the grim realities of human life'.[16] But is that not what fairy-tales usually do? The community of ants is extremely hierarchical and tyrannical, be it at the Home Ants' or at the Garden Ants'. Any transgression, or mere aspiration to independence might be severely punished, which underlines the tension between the individual and the community, repeatedly emphasized in Frame's fiction. To be/long or not to be/long is the question. Wanting to get out of the nest might be rewarding and part of one's initiation and experience, but it is also dangerous and even self-destructive. Mona could have been killed in her fall, could have been blinded by a very ambiguous sun (*MM* 10), had not Barbara, the Garden Ant, come to the rescue and found her: 'I am found [...] and you are lost' (*MM* 20), as if they were property. The French translation for 'Lost Property' happens to be: 'Objets trouvés' (found objects). Could Frame's pun be bilingual? The meeting between the two ants who belong to the two antagonistic 'antdoms' could be read as a rewriting of La Fontaine's 'The town mouse and the country mouse' whose life-styles are totally different. But it also echoes Frame's own story 'Keel and Kool' where the two girls Joan and Winnie exchange their respective experiences: not unlike Scheherazade, Mona wins her right to enter the 'other' place, thanks to her narration of the fascinating Stair Game (*MM* 21). But *Mona Minim* is also, and not unexpectedly, a story of difference, expressed in terms of smell. As a child, Mona had been told the exemplary story of cousin Bruno, 'who had been caught and killed by his own family simply because he was wearing a different smell in his clothing' (*MM* 5–6). Mona is faced with the same problem on two different occasions when Barbara has to spray Garden-Ant scent on her to introduce her into her new family and when she goes back home, like an 'illegal immigr*ant*' (*MM* 118; author's italics). Frame constantly, and somewhat systematically, plays on words containing the syllable 'ant', such as 'inf*ant*ile', '*ant*icipate', '*ant*hology', 'flipp*ant*', 'f*ant*astic', 'dist*ant*', to quote but a few. The community is guarded by sentinels and functions on the same model as Mona's former place. Aunt Phyllis, the soldier ant, is the Garden Ant version of Aunt Theodora: it is signific*ant* (italics mine) that the Aunts should play the part of surrogate mothers, as if (as was often the case in African villages) they were entrusted with the children's education. The other members of the family are Nigel and Uncle Pogo, the storyteller, who tells Mona her own story twice (*MM* 37 and 73), in an echo to the impostor novelist, Dinny Wheatstone in *The Carpathians* who tells Mattina, the American woman, her own story. 'The same story, which remains unfinished and precipitates Mona into a brooding mood at the thought that, this being her tale, she will have to complete it by herself'.[17] Mona learns to work, to teach – she lectures on House Ants – but pines for home, where she plans to return 'Some Day' (*MM* 59). The capturing of several ants by Peter, the boy of the house, who 'swept them into a huge glass building' (*MM* 64) triggers Mona's decision to try and rescue her friend Barbara, who is among the prisoners. Panic and violence follow the capturing: George the baker, a usually placid ant, kills his nephew. But as in *The Carpathians*, after the disappearance of the whole street, everything is back to normal 'in a flash', 'as if nothing had happened' (*MM* 66), as in the dystopic world of *Intensive Care*. Mona might be brave, 'but not too brave' (*MM* 147). She is torn between the desire to save her friend and to appear heroic, and her frivolous preoccupation with clothes.

When she first went out of the nest, Aunt Theodora had advised her not to wear her best floral apron and her six black-buttoned shoes because the smell was unusual. In the Autobiography, Frame remembers how uneasy she felt when her mother wore her best coat to come and visit her, as if she were no longer her usual self. What is at stake here, be it the different smell or the different clothes, is the impossibility of recognizing the other, or accepting him or her as other. The other is acceptable, and accepted only if he or she looks, smells and behaves like you.

On her expedition to save Barbara, Mona means to take along her '*ant*ennae brush and a change of clothing and [her] six red resting-slippers and her sunbonnet' (*MM* 83–4; author's italics), which seems, as Mona is well aware, incompatible with heroism: 'How can you make such dreams come true if you can't even decide whether to take your sunbonnet and your six red-resting slippers'? (*MM* 87). She finally decides to leave on the festive Day of the Princess. On her solitary way, she meets Princess Antonia, who has broken one of her wings and requires Mona's help to pull off the other. With this meeting, Mona loses some of her illusions: the Queen is not what she had imagined she would be. She is callous and unhappy. Wallace, her husband, will die 'because he won the race' (*MM* 106) as if that were the price to pay to have access to knowledge: 'He would know and not know just as I knew and didn't know' (*MM* 107), though this certainty is undermined at the very moment of its utterance. The Queen gives Mona an anklet that will guide her in her journey back home. On her arrival back at the House Ants, Mona has to prove her identity, trying to explain to the soldiers why she has 'different', 'imported' clothes. One of the soldiers' answer is just another example of Frame's incorrigible taste for word-play: 'That melts no honey with us' (*MM* 121). It is only when Mona recalls the Stair Game that her former friend Pamela, now a soldier, finally remembers her. She is even greeted as a heroine, the prodigal Mona, who has survived a tragic fall. As for Barbara, she is now a Princess, and soon to become a Queen. And *she* 'know[s] the smell of the blue in the sky, of the wind that never comes close to earth grass but blows' (*MM* 141). In her final day-dreaming, Mona retraces her own story: 'Once upon a time, not long ago, almost now' (*MM* 145). She has now become a wise old ant, who has accumulated experience, which she can transmit in her turn. Mona remembers the Big Queen's advice: 'see and smell and hear and touch for yourself what it means' (*MM* 96). Significantly, the last word of the book is 'know' (*MM* 148).

Mona's initial fall was a fall from innocence into experience, and songs of experience are often painful ones. But that is also the price she has to pay to know the smell of the sun.

TOWARDS ANOTHER SUMMER: A POSTHUMOUS 'AUTOBIOGRAFICTIONAL WORK'

Towards Another Summer is a novella written in 1963 but published posthumously in 2007. Grace is the heroine of this novel in which autobiography crops up on almost every page, in the form of nostalgic reminiscences triggered by situations or events, not unlike Proust's madeleine.[18] The narrative alternates between past and present, and, like the Autobiography, it is written in a realistic mode, apart from Grace's 'flights of fancy' when she transforms herself into a migratory bird. The image of the bird is recurrent in the poems, in the short stories, but also in the Autobiography where, after having been divested of her 'schizophrenic fancy dress', Janet perceives herself as an 'ordinary grey-feathered bird' (II 81).

As a writer exiled in Great Britain, Grace has been invited to spend a weekend in the north by the journalist who had interviewed her, Philip, and his family. The preparations for the weekend, and even more so, the stay itself, represent almost insurmountable obstacles for extremely shy Grace, who has none of the social graces expected in one who is so good at writing: 'daring, imaginative, witty letters that reveal nothing of her social stupidity!' (*TAS* 91). In his biography on Frame, Michael King quotes John Money in a letter to the Maudsley doctor: 'It is unique in my experience to find such a split between written lucidity and oral muteness, a muteness that becomes sheer panic on many occasions, when Miss Frame has to enter into conversation, especially with strangers' (*WA* 181). As she says in the Autobiography, the most problematic aspect of life is to be able to satisfy the expectations of others. Philip, in particular, seems disappointed that she should not be more talkative, that she should be at a loss for what to say or what to do. Grace herself has the feeling that she is always saying the wrong things at the wrong moment: she is painfully aware of her deficiencies in human relations, of her fear of others, who threaten to invade her privacy. She can hardly believe that Philip lets her enter his study: 'How could he dare to give a stranger permission to enter this room!' (*TAS* 170).

The idea that there are two children in the family terrifies her at first: 'the most frightening thing in the world was a child standing, not speaking, staring at her, staring accusingly, knowingly, pityingly' (*TAS* 44). In a letter to John Money, Frame had written: 'I am a snail [...] But I am easily frightened' (*WA* 68). Feeling excluded from this closely-knit family, she confuses Anne with her mother, as, like her, she is so committed to domestic duties: 'As she watched Anne going about her task of preparing tea [...] Grace had a strange feeling that Anne was her mother, about to "dish up" for the family, and that she was a child sitting at the big wooden table' (*TAS* 120). Actually, both Philip and Anne become Grace's parents: 'You see, they are my mother and father' (*TAS* 128), to the point that Grace fears violence between them as she did as a child if her mother ever dared to contradict her father, or simply express an opinion: 'Let them not kill each other' (*TAS* 127). But the past is also a source of happiness and comfort that Grace needs to recreate in order to survive.

Home, however messy it might have been, was still her place, with 'roots of love in the wild untidy blossoming' (*TAS* 50). The sense of place is paramount in all of Frame's works: 'So I, a migratory bird, am suffering from the need to return to the place I have come from' (*TAS* 59). Grace gives us a sense of the numerous places she has lived in: Glenham (*TAS* 73), Edendale (*TAS* 74), Wyndham (*TAS* 75) and finally Oamaru (*TAS* 175). In the Autobiography, Janet says that she had 'an exaggerated sense of movement' (I 43) and whenever she moved, she tried to find 'a place of her own': 'I knew, with a surge of pleasure inside me, that I had set out to look for my place, and that I had found it, that I had chosen it' (*TAS* 60; author's italics). But a place of one's own also entails solitude and isolation: 'I cannot describe the sense of loneliness I felt when I knew that I was in my place' (*TAS* 59). The feeling of exclusion is not exclusively aroused by the 'other' country. Janet/Grace's life is a story of difference. Grace feels uncomfortable in her clothes: 'and suddenly my clothes were too small' (*TAS* 180), which echoes how the school tunic was too tight for Janet; Grace also feels her hair is wrong: 'people in the street stopped to stare at it' (*TAS* 121), and is embarrassed by her (wrong) brother: 'Jimmy was sick, too, in the middle of the night' (*TAS* 180). It is thanks to poetry that she is able to 'reconnect': 'All the poets are writing about *my* place' (*TAS* 61; author's italics). On this point, Alice Braun quotes Charles Brash: 'New Zealand lived in me as no other country could live, part of myself as I was part of it, the world I breathed and wore from birth, my seeing and my language'.[19] Grace's mother sees *poetry* as 'an effective revenge against *poverty*' (*TAS* 123; italics mine); at home the songs her father sang about the war made them cry (*TAS* 78). The impression the First World War had made on Grace was so profound that it was as if she had lived through it herself. In *Intensive Care*, the first part is also centred on the war, too, and its aftermath. The war is something Grace shares with her father, like crosswords, with the epiphanic discovery of the word *'rattan*' (*TAS* 122) or the '"jewl" desks' (*TAS* 178; JF's spelling) that used to puzzle Turnlung in *Daughter Buffalo*. Even more than any of the other novels, *Towards Another Summer* seems to be a generic hybrid, at the crossroads between fiction and autobiography. The episode at the dentist's where Grace/Janet experiences the treachery of words for the first time is related at length in both the novella and the Autobiography as if she had needed to rehearse before the final show. The other landmark in Grace's life is the 'thief episode' (*TAS* 157) which is related at length in the Autobiography. Whereas the 'God save our gracious tin' (*TAS* 72) is given equal treatment in both works.

At the end of the novella, Grace takes on her migratory bird identity again to fly away from her well-meaning hosts and like the early bird she has always prided herself (*TAS* 47; 201) on being, she catches her train.

5

An Angel at My Table

TO THE IS-LAND

The writing of an autobiography might seem surprising in Frame's case as she was sent to a psychiatric hospital on the strength of an autobiographical essay in which she had related a suicide attempt. She could have developed a legitimate distrust for a genre that had cost her so much. However, the Autobiography can also be read as the revenge of an 'I' that had been silenced for so long: 'with the autobiography it was the desire really to make myself a first person'[1] Frame says in one of the rare interviews she gave. For years – between twenty and thirty – she was a non-person, sharing the lot of children and mad people who are forever 'they' or the alienating, destroying third person.

The trilogy is built along the lines of a *Bildungsroman* – 'The Sorrows of Janet Frame'[2] – in that it follows the heroine/narrator/author from her birth till the age of 40 or so. Frame seems to abide by the 'autobiographical pact' as defined by Lejeune: author, narrator and character must be one and the same. But like any autobiographer, she also subverts some of the rules, giving her own definition of an autobiography: 'Writing an autobiography, usually thought of as a looking back, can just as well be a looking *across* or *through*, with the passing of time giving an X-ray quality to the eye' (II 67; JF's italics). According to Gisèle Mathieu-Castellani in her book *La Scène Judiciaire de l'Autobiographie*,[3] metatextual commentaries are part and parcel of autobiographical writing.

Volume I hinges on the discovery of – and passion for – words that brings to light Frame's wish to become a writer together with a feeling of difference that works both ways: either as a handicap or as a prestigious aura. The first leads her to a psychiatric hospital and constitutes the subject matter of the second volume, whereas the second is linked to creation: the 'mad woman' has become a famous artist. The title of volume I of the Autobiography, is *To The Is-land*, but it could also have echoed Jean-Paul Sartre's own Autobiography entitled 'Words',[4] as it focuses essentially on Janet Frame's fascination and taste for words. At the beginning were words. It is said that she had written her first poem at the age of three: 'Once upon a time there was a bird. One day a hawk came out of the sky and ate the bird. The next day a big bogie came out from behind the hill and ate up the hawk for eating up the bird'.[5] Every experience is linked to a word. One of the most striking examples is the discovery of the word 'fuck' with its dramatic consequences when Janet declares in the face of her incredulous family: 'Myrtle and Ted did it in the plannies this afternoon' (I 56), before transforming a prudent 'did' into a more explicit 'fuck', and as a result, she is punished for having uttered such a taboo word as severely as Myrtle is for 'having done it'. The word amounts to the deed. And Janet Frame's father, playing the traditional part of father in the no less traditional society of New Zealand in the 1950s means to educate his children in the right way with the help of a whip. He also wields it on his epileptic son, as he is convinced Bruddie could stop his fits if he wanted to. Illness is as taboo as sex, unless sex may be considered as an illness, too. If Janet's father's remedy is physical, the mother's strategies in the field of taboos are verbal: she is a champion in the art of clichés and euphemisms, 'beating about the words' in sometimes comic ways. One such instance is when she announces in her 'earthquake' voice that 'Myrtle's come, Myrtle's come' (I 57), meaning she has her periods, but leading Janet down a far more taboo track!

The word *morgue* is also taboo at home, as if uttering it could make death come true. It is only and ironically when Myrtle drowns in the local swimming pool that the children are allowed to utter the words 'death' or 'die', because 'the thing' has at last happened and there is no need to fear its 'actualization' any longer. When Isabel, the other sister, dies, drowned too, a few years later, in a kind of tragic repetition, Janet receives a telegram from John Forrest, her much admired university lecturer, whose contents shock her for the conventionality of its language: if the mother may be forgiven for her use of clichés and euphemisms because she is not educated, John Forrest does not have the same excuses. 'Money himself now wrote what Janet would judge to be another "form letter" [...] Frame [...] made no allowance for the difficulties people experienced trying to respond to death' (WA 89). Frame gives the supremacy to *parole* – the sign of individuality – over *langue* – the social use of language – which is exemplified in her poetic tastes. This distinction is evident in the episode I have already quoted of the poem which was a bone of contention between Myrtle and Janet (I 83).

Frame's rebellion is textual: she means to free language from its straitjacket of conventionality. She means to acquire 'a language of her own'. The very title of the first volume of the trilogy, *To The Is-Land*, with its significant hyphen, is a typographic rendering of Janet's mispronunciation of the word. The first time she comes upon the word *island* is a sort of spelling epiphany. She refuses to abide by the rules of silent letters, a rule that she will have to suffer from as an individual reduced to the silence of 'the mad', referring to those who should not be given any right to speak. If the word *island* is spelt with an 'S', this 'S' should, in her childish logic, be pronounced. And against her elder sister's advice, she obstinately clings to this theory, going as far as to publish her first volume under this title as a kind of revenge for the customary silence to which the S had been condemned. The wrong spelling of the word polysemizes it: it becomes the land of the *I* or the land of the present, of the *Now* as opposed to her ancestors' 'Was-Land' (I 13). The caesura opens up a multitude of semantic fields: by changing its pronunciation, Frame changes the very concept and the word becomes like Pandora's box, offering the readers as many interpretations as they wish, without giving any of them supremacy over any other. The very word is in itself an adventure.[6] Frame will even change its nature when she turns it into an adjective used to qualify her friend's family: 'the almost island state of their family' (I 169). Words are magic. By rebaptizing 'Ferry Street', 'Fairy Street', she typographically and semantically actualizes this magic power. All the Frame children are hungry for words and the climax of happiness is when they can literalize their passion by devouring the icing set on the Christmas cake: 'Words and phrases that could be eaten!' (I 96). Frame extols the cohabitation of the written and the real worlds, in anticipation of her apprehension of the world as 'this' (the *hic et nunc*) and 'that' world, the world of imagination, Mirror City. Despite her barely hidden contempt for her mother who is immersed in her domestic chores, Frame nonetheless recognizes that she owes her gift for poetry to this very same mother who is a surprising mixture of matter-of-factness and poetry: 'When mother talked of the present, however, bringing her sense of wondrous contemplation to the ordinary world we knew, we listened, feeling the mystery and the magic. She had only to say of any commonplace object, 'Look, kiddies, a stone', to fill that stone with a wonder as if it were a holy object' (I 12).

It is as if the mother were endowed with a gift of transfiguration, transsubstantiation even. This 'miracle' is developed in Frame's fiction *Owls Do Cry* where the rubbish dump is a place for treasures, such as old books. The miracle is also performed through the tone given to words, 'sensing the feeling behind people's words', as when her father speaks of his Maori friend and of his daughter who is 'only a half-caste' (I 67); the restrictive 'only' preceding the mysterious 'half-caste' invites the child Janet to conjecture that the girl might not enjoy the integrity of her being. Janet is a word-taster who spends her time trying to decipher the adults' puzzling codes. The title of chapter 10, 'OK Permanent Wave' (I 60), is a comic though significant example: Janet cannot be reconciled to the idea that words do not mean what they appear to mean. There is an obvious breach between signifier and signified. If one needs second 'permanent waves', what is the true meaning of 'permanent'? What puzzles her even more is people's general indifference in front of such a betrayal. This example partakes of the comic, but later on in her life, this inadequacy between signifier and signified takes on far more dramatic aspects. When Janet Frame realizes she is being taken to a psychiatric hospital, it is after having heard the apparently innocuous words: 'We thought you would like to have a little rest' (II 64). Hence the mixed feelings she has for words which she both cherishes and dreads. 'How could a few kind words mean so much harm?' (I 29) is Janet's question when, as a child at the dentist's, she is put to sleep by these other very innocent sounding words: 'Smell the pretty pink towel' (I 29). It will be very difficult and painful for her to accept the deceit of words, like a lover who cannot bring him/herself to accept her/his beloved's betrayal.

Wanting to become a writer could even be read as a kind of revenge for the past betrayals. She writes 'with words of her own', the words she chooses and not those that had been imposed upon her. The first volume is a hymn to words, whose discovery coincides with childhood. And most of Frame's discoveries are real epiphanies: 'Spoken words in childhood, arrive from 'on high' – as high as the sky –'.[7] When she helps her father with his crosswords, finding the word 'rattan' is a source of infinite happiness. Words are first tasted individually before coalescing into texts and books and fostering her taste for writing.

This first volume is also concerned with Janet's own self, her sense of identity (a question that is all the more acute in postcolonial writings) as her repeated allusions to the body testify. Her body is constantly preying on her mind. In my introduction, I wrote that women's autobiographies were more preoccupied with the body than men's and Frame's work strengthens that point. Her 'legs like footballers' legs, and wristbones that reminded me of railway sleepers' (III 74) are perceived as severe handicaps on the marriage market. Frame's humorous perception of her body is all the more acute as she grows older and is worried about her belated virginity. One of her main concerns is her red bushy hair that draws attention to her which she would rather avoid: 'to be in a sense, invisible' (I 122) is her main wish. Throughout the trilogy, the mention of her hair appears almost as a symptom. It grows upwards 'inexcusably really',[8] 'with everyone remarking on it' (I 82). Difference is only perceived as such because 'the others' make you feel it, because of the social gaze. Frame is even convinced her Grandma was African, one of the colonized peoples. 'Throughout history, hair has taken on cultural significance as a symbol of difference and has been employed to represent idealized versions of class, race and gender both by the dominant and the oppressed'.[9] For Frame, hair epitomizes otherness. In volume III of the Autobiography, she tries to have it flattened, ironed out, to (literally) 'smooth the surface of life' (I 122). Frame stands in an uncomfortable in-betweenness, on the cusp of whiteness and blackness: 'No one had [hair like me] except Fijian and African people in faraway lands' (I 138). She will suffer multiple forms of ostracization, of exclusion, that may reflect her own country's distance from the rest of the world, especially Europe: *'all the way from New Zealand'* (III 18; author's italics). Her/story and history are closely linked for a post-colonial author writing '[from] the rim of the farthest circle' (I 117). Her social 'estrangement'– she is the daughter of a poor railway worker – entails but another form of suffering. Her clothes, like her hair, are never right. 'Clothes are crucial symbols of wealth, femininity and belonging'.[10] Throughout the Autobiography, clothes, which are at the crossroads between the social and the personal, take on a particular significance, especially the school tunic which was too tight and imperfect from the start, with its two pleats instead of the customary three. Whereas a uniform should erase difference, in Frame's case on the contrary it only contributes to enhance it. But after years of wearing it, and when she has to give it up to go to university, she feels 'naked, like a skinned rabbit' (I 171), as if she were being deprived of part of herself, of a second skin, a helpful hide to hide in and even an identity.

The feeling will recur in exactly the same terms when the diagnosis of schizophrenia is invalidated in London: it is as if she had lost an identity to which she had grown accustomed. Clothes play the part of protective layers, not unlike schizophrenia, the illness she first hates before deciding to adopt it, to make it a powerful ally in her artistic creation and the mark of her identity. It is significant that the first volume should end on clothes in the form of an impressive list she has to buy to enter university. Frame feels entitled to prune the list as if so many clothes were forbidden fruit it would be a sin to have. In London, the psychiatrist she meets at the Maudsley Hospital wears an impressive number of clothes, which seems to literalize the association between illness and clothes. Frame's sensitivity to clothes is as paradoxical as most of her attitudes and reactions: she both wishes she had more, or rather the right kind, but each time her parents put on their best ones to visit her in hospital or attend a ceremony, she feels threatened as if a change in one's clothes meant a change in one's identity, which confirms the equation between self and clothes as second skin:

'In a life where people had few clothes and a man one suit and one overcoat, the clothes were part of the skin, like an animal's fur' (I 171).

What is at stake in this first volume is Frame's difference, a difference that is social and physical, but also mental. But this difference can and will diverge in opposite directions developed in the two following volumes of the trilogy: the second one focuses, though elliptically, on Frame's repeated stays in psychiatric hospitals – and this is the first negative invalidating kind of difference – whereas the third and last one consecrates her as the prestigious writer she has become: difference also means prestige. It is as if Frame were actualizing her mother's syllogistical creed, which she tried to instil in her epileptic son's mind: difference is a sign of genius. Julius Caesar was epileptic and he became famous. Bruddie Frame is also epileptic: he will no doubt become famous. As with the Brontës, it is the sister who supplants the brother, her own handicap 'qualifying' her just as efficaciously for the prestige.

The first volume also ends with attempts at signing her name, at finding the best correspondence between her self and this name. 'The subject of an autobiography is one's own name'.[11] A signature is the graphic mark of the self. By inserting 'Paterson' between her first name and her last, she seems to be giving the full measure of her new found identity. By trying to define a new self, she discards all the old nicknames she had as a child, as if they were so many worn-out clothes or borrowed identities: 'The old Nini and Fuzzy and Jean being discarded' (I 172). Throughout the book, she is playing with a multiplicity of different selves she either finds herself or others find for her. Even though she is writing an autobiography, Frame refuses to abide by the pact of 'telling the whole truth'. She goes as far as to declare (but only at the end of the third volume) to a puzzled reader who is, he/she thinks entitled to expect 'the truth' at last: 'I've created "selves", but I've never written of "me"' (III 154), which seems to contradict the declaration she had made in an interview: 'In *To The Is-land*, I wrote the story of my life, My story, and this is me which comes out. There is pain, things happen, but whatever comes out is ordinary me without fiction or characters'.[12] Her playing with her different selves entails playing with the reader, as if she were 'leading him up the garden path'. This game, however, only reinforces Frame's conviction that autobiography and fiction are but one and the same, which also sustains my own theory: there is autobiography in her fiction and vice versa. No autobiographer can write a 'pure' autobiography, none can escape generic hybridity. Her self is to be found in both or not found at all, and in fact what matters most is her writing. As she relates in the first volume, she goes from one self to another as much as she moves places. The self is to be built geographically, which will be illustrated even more convincingly in the third volume when Frame leaves New Zealand to travel to Europe. Her different transient selves are like clothes she would try on and reject when they no longer suit her. In the second volume she speaks of her 'schizophrenic fancy dress' (II 81) which she wears on special occasions. Janet Frame is Nini at home, a childish nickname, and Jean at school. Could so many names be a sign of riches, abundance or fragmentation? Are they not a kind of compensation for somebody who is 'desperately looking for her self'? In Ibiza, her Spanish hostesses baptize her 'Escritora' and this baptism will have a performative role: she is said to be a writer and she will actually become one but in her own country, refusing to be – like so many others – a writer in exile. As a child, with her brother and sisters, and like the Brontë children she often evokes, she dreams of being famous, or an actress or singer. 'THE FRAME SISTERS THOUGHT OF THEMSELVES AS BRONTËS: BECAUSE they held, by right, "silk purses of words";' (*WA Prologue*; author's capitals). Frame tried 'many aspects of being: a giggling school-girl who made everyone laugh with comic recitations, mimicry, puzzles, mathematical tricks [...] attempts at ventriloquism' (I 136–7). The main character/narrator in *Living in the Maniototo* is a ventriloquist. There is one significant episode at the beginning of volume I when Frame, who has stolen some money from her father's pocket to buy chewing gum for all her class-mates, is punished by the school teacher but refuses to confess. But 'a small voice answered from the scared me' (I 32), prompting her into telling the truth and making her lose the protection of the lie: 'While I'd been lying, I had somehow protected myself; I knew now that I had no protection' (I 32). The truth is more dangerous than the lie, as it 'exposes' the self, and autobiography is more dangerous than fiction. Frame believes in make-believe, a creed she will develop and apply for years behind the mask of the schizophrenic. Her wish to be invisible goes hand in hand with a pathological shyness, reinforced by a physical appearance she has difficulties in accepting, a social status that sets her apart from the prestigious Group of girls at school, in a word a difference that is not tolerated in a society whose motto is, as the teacher inculcates in the girls: 'to be in step always' (I 113). This difference, however embarrassing it may be for a child, takes on some far more dramatic aspects when, as a young adult – she was 20 at the time – Frame is diagnosed with schizophrenia.

AN ANGEL AT MY TABLE

Like most of Frame's experiences, the discovery of the illness is also linked to a word she hears for the first time. After having rushed out of the classroom in front of a school inspector, Frame writes an essay relating an attempt at suicide that alerts her university lecturers. The episode is dramatized in *Faces in the Water* where Frame humorously writes 'a triple peril followed me' (FW 11) in a sinister parody of the divine trinity. As in childhood, but far more tragically, Frame is confronted with the destroying power of words that have betrayed her. The three lecturers invite her to 'have a little rest' (II 64) hiding the terrible reality under some apparently innocuous words. For eight years, Frame experiences a real descent into the Hell of psychiatric hospitals, which she portrays in graphic detail in her fiction and more particularly in *Faces in the Water*, refusing to sound 'overdramatic' in the Autobiography. It is indeed striking that she should devote only seven chapters to those traumatizing years. The diagnosis falls like a sentence in Frame's life as the definition leaves little room for optimism: 'A disease without hope' (II 75). However, and this is also characteristic of her imaginative talent, Frame misspells it: *shizzofreenier*, turning the *phre* into a significant *free*, thereby making the illness a possible ally in her creation and a space of freedom. Like her difference, her illness is both a terrible handicap and a bane, but also a gift, and a boon. It is 'the gift of the loss' (III 19) as she herself puts it on her arrival in London, where her booking letter has not reached its destination but where she experiences a sort of literary epiphany. Since she has been diagnosed schizophrenic, she will play the part, which she does in her informal therapy sessions with John Forrest, applying her newly discovered psychoanalytical theories, like 'a textbook schizophrenic' (II 81), fulfilling his expectations by conforming to the image he has of her, by abiding (as usual) by the new rules of her new 'status'. He easily falls into the trap she lays for him, going as far as to reproduce typographically the hesitations she knows she should have before confessing the 'sin' of masturbation: 'It's masturbation, worry over masturbation...' (II 81), the dots augmenting the suspense and shame linked to the alliance of two taboos: illness and sex. But pretending to be mad could be a dangerous game that may lead to real madness. And she is so good at it that one could be mistaken; and many have indeed been, since: 'Performing is as good as the real thing (one of the symptoms of schizophrenia is indeed the performance of symptoms of schizophrenia). While her text is still inescapably bound to the logos and while she is evidently in control of her narrative, the text nevertheless conveys the pathos of madness: performs madness without being it.'[13] She 'becomes' schizophrenic because she has been told she is, once more playing the part of the obedient, 'no trouble at all' girl (II 56), 'the textbook schizophrenic' (II 81).

Frame specializes in the art of reverting, inverting and changing the situations and the whole Autobiography is a perfect illustration of this incredible skill or adaptability. Frame is one of the fittest who owes her survival to this talent. Incredible though it may appear, schizophrenia becomes her identity, an identity she has always been looking for: better mad than nothing. But the image of herself she has inside and outside the hospital is totally different: if her schizophrenia endows her with the prestige her mother links with invalidating illnesses, inside the hospital she experiences a general feeling of self-erasure: 'I was a nothing and nobody' (II 110), punished for the crime of difference. To resume and sum up Foucault's[14] analyses: 'Mad is bad'. She undergoes a slow but sure process of disidentification that could have culminated in a lobotomy, as the ultimate step to annihilation. The world of the mad is now the world she belongs to: the rim she had alluded to in the first volume is even 'furtherized' and the alienation is complete. The insane 'had no legal or personal identity' (II 69), 'nothing left but a nickname with even the word *nick*name hinting at the presence of devils' (II 70; author's italics). Her difference is absorbed in similarity and in a terrifying uniformity. It is significant that Frame's metaphors are spatial, relating to countries, territories and places, as the expression of her acute personal need for 'a place of her own'.

Throughout the trilogy, the signifier 'place' recurs obsessively, linking Frame's own destiny to her country's, a dominion under British rule. Her eloquent coinage 'homelessness of self' (I 136)[15] in the first volume is not only a personal dilemma (though it obviously is that as well, to a dangerous degree in her case) but it is also the dilemma of a country depending on another like a child on his parents. We know to what extent colonized countries and peoples are infantilized by their colonizers. New Zealand takes its models from Great Britain, be it in educational, cultural or social fields. At the end of the second volume, Janet's father, who has come to say goodbye, calls Great Britain 'home'. Janet's need for appropriation of the different places she lives or spends time in can appear frightful in the case of the hospital she calls 'my adopted country' (II 99). The reader has always been puzzled by this desperate wish to fit in at any cost, to the point even of refusing to follow her mother 'home' and of preferring to stay in hospital. Frame never seems to rebel against her situation, as if she had been deprived of all her fighting spirit, or as if she had finally accepted that 'they' may have been right in the diagnosis. The use of the indefinite 'they' is all the more destabilizing as it is indefinite. Or may this passivity be expressive of a form of relief? The relief of having found at last the 'home' she had been looking for, together with the identity she had never managed to find in the 'normal' world, the world outside that stigmatizes and punishes anything different?

The 'home', however, looks far from welcoming. It is more like a prison of the Inquisition, a gothic fortress 'a castle of dark stone between the hills' (II 13) and the patients are more like prisoners in a camp. Janet's description of the men in striped shirts and trousers evokes convicts rather than patients in a hospital. The place is also terrifyingly evocative of a huge coffin, as the patients are often forgotten by their relatives, as if they were dead: 'Few people have advance glimpses of their coffin' (*FW* 24) she writes in *Faces in the Water*. Seacliff is the punishment inflicted on those who have disobeyed by infringing the laws of normality, on those who have dared to be different. It warrants the isolation and separation between the 'mad' and the sane, as if the mad could contaminate the sane. And for fear of appearing too mad in the eyes of her 'normal' relatives, Frame relates her stays at Seacliff as if they were a holiday, resorting to what Gina Mercer calls linguistic 'strategies of avoidance', such as paralepsis:[16] 'I didn't tell them how I had peeped through the fence of a building called *Simla* [...] where there were strange men in striped shirts and trousers and some without trousers [...] and I didn't say how there was a special section for the patients with tuberculosis' (II 71; author's italics); or humour: 'I described only the amusing incidents and the stereotypes of patients – the Jesus Christ, the Queen, the Empress' (II 101) as for a fancy dress party where she, too, can wear her cherished 'schizophrenic fancy dress' (II 81).

The more, the merrier. The hospital is a joyous, happy world peopled with funny citizens. Frame 'beats about words' for fear that a realistic description might convince the 'normal' people that she is really mad since she has been sent to such a place. 'An excess of reality can drive one mad' says Claude Burgelin in a collection of essays on autobiography.[17] Frame hides the reality of hospital life from her family but she lets the reader in on the secret. At home, as the 'acknowledged misfit' (II 101), she is excluded from the 'normal' women's conversations, which cannot but intensify her difference. Her family is like the microscosm of New Zealand itself, a conformist society that abhors difference and condemns it. The circle is vicious indeed. People search for stigmata of madness, for tell-tale signs: 'She's been in Seacliff' (II 74).

The punishment for the crime of difference is first the series of electro-convulsive therapy sessions, which are the equivalent in pain of an assassination and the modern version of the stake according to Mercer. What should come next as the panacea is the lobotomy which Mercer analyses in the following way: 'The authorities seek to eliminate even this secret crevice of treasure through a lobotomy' (*SF* 36). Daphne, the heroine of *Owls Do Cry* does have her lobotomy and it is ironically only after this miraculous operation that she is given a place in society as she works in a factory. Daphne is inspired by the character of Nola in the Autobiography (herself based on the real Audrey Scrivener) (WA 113), who, says Frame, 'unfortunately had not won a prize' (II 109). Frame's humour turns black when she reinscribes the taboo subject of illness in her writing and attacks a society that has almost destroyed her. 'Black humour is the revolt of superior minds' wrote the French surrealist author André Breton.[18]

Frame escapes the lobotomy thanks to the publication of her first collection of short stories, *The Lagoon*, which won the Hubert Church Award, thus drawing the attention of the surgeon who was about to perform the operation. Hence Frame's boundless and eternal gratitude towards writing. On coming out of hospital her first movement is to have her photo taken as if she meant to prove she was still alive. Photos do play a significant part in her life to the point that the latest edition of the Autobiography (where the three parts are collected together in one single volume) contains a number of photographs aiming, perhaps, at authenticating the autobiographical writing. They also reflect the modern tendency to 'mediatize' famous people by adding new documents to the original text so as to widen the autobiographical scope and to sell the book better. In Frame's case, the insertion of photographs might also be a dilatory response to Myrtle's 'ghost photo' where, on a family picnic, the girl had not appeared in the picture, a harbinger, maybe, of her impending death: 'Mother gave a gasp of horror when she saw that in one of the photographs Myrtle appeared to be transparent' (I 105). Frame seems to believe in the power of photos to resurrect the dead or to prolong their lives, and thus adheres to a common enough creed that might need re-examining in the light of Roland Barthes and Susan Sontag's[19] theories about the very ambiguous status of photographs that tend to fix their objects in a mock eternity, in a word to 'kill' or rather 'shoot' them.

This theory can apply to the analysis of the short story 'Keel and Kool' in particular. In this short story which is a fictionalization of Myrtle's death, the sympathizing neighbours comfort the mother with the usual cliché (the word also means photograph in French): 'You've got her photo' (*La* 20), as if photos could compensate for the loss, even replace the dead girl, whose death is also reduced to a euphemism as the mother never says 'died', but 'passed away' or 'gone', as if euphemism were a remedy to alleviate the pain. As for Janet, she struggles against the petrifying power of clichés (even if she herself resorts to them when it suits her) especially when applied in the taboo fields of illness, sex and death, the sacred (the Latin word *sacer* means both sacred and impure) objects of ancestral fears. When Janet has her photo taken after the stay in hospital – the place of illness and death – she says that her finished portrait 'showed a healthy young woman with obvious false teeth, a smirking smile [...] Well, I was alive again' (II 130). Herself 'with a difference'. The obvious false teeth are (surprisingly enough) but another token of conformity: '(The general opinion in New Zealand then was that natural teeth were best removed anyway, it was a kind of *colonial* squandering, like the needless uprooting of forests)' (II 80; italics mine; author's parenthesis). They mark another alteration to her body, like the advice to straighten her rebellious mop, and all these measures serve to illustrate and enforce the same deeply-anchored creed: difference is a threat in a conformist society where it must be either corrected (with the help of drastic remedies) or totally annihilated.

However, schizophrenia, the terrible illness Janet is supposed to suffer from, is paradoxically also a refuge, like the hospital itself, 'both a trap' and 'a refuge' (II 96). Frame's spelling distorts the word, so that the syllable *free* is so to speak actualized by Frame herself. She decides to use her illness as a protective shield but also as a mark of genius: 'I could endow my work, and – when necessary my life – with the mark of my schizophrenia' (II 79), a token of difference but of a prestigious difference, that of artists, of poets, prophets and visionaries. 'My only hope was to write [...] the long essay in my own way, that is to attach my own giraffe [her sister Isabel had sown one on her skirt and was punished for it at college] to the ordinary garb of prose' (II 44–5; my parenthesis). We have already seen that Simone Oettli-van Delden denounces this systematic association in Frame's works where she seems to equate illness (mental or physical) with genius, as if only the 'handicapped', or the 'different' could have access to a superior vision, as if also she were actualizing her mother's own comforting conviction that 'difference' is necessarily a mark of genius. Frame's schizophrenia becomes her second skin or 'the mantle of difference' (I 136) she dons with pride, like a prize she would have won. Frame does on occasion reveal her feelings of superiority, for example when she works as maid in a hotel and declares: 'I felt like a secret princess among the scullions' (II 117), a reiteration of her refusal to follow the literary dictatorship of the Group at school (the Group is also at the core of the short story 'Hecate, You Look Angerly' in *The Reservoir*), because, though she was poor, she was also the best pupil. She welcomes the illness, courts it to the unbelievable point that when the diagnosis is invalidated in London, she feels as naked as when she had to give up her worn out school tunic. She experiences a kind of amputation: 'I could never again turn to it for help' (III 116). She is now exposed in all the ordinariness of 'a grey-feathered bird' (II 81), her true self. The fear of ordinariness is harped on and could account for Frame's desperate wish or effort to be different, even if the cost is very high. But this self is also capable of producing the works of art we know.

She gradually accepts this emerging self which the trips and stays abroad help (re)construct. Frame's biography is a geography. Temporary exile is necessary to achieve the process of creation that had started at home but had been seriously threatened. 'Exile is the shortest way to oneself'.[20] After her release from hospital, Frame spends some time in Frank Sargeson's hut,[21] free to write and live as she wishes. It is at Sargeson's that she also learns the virtues of tolerance for those who are different in ways which differ from her(s). Frank and his friends are homosexuals, another 'marginal' community Frame had never met: 'I was repelled by the idea of both male and female homosexuality yet I was learning slowly to accept the sacred differences in people although I was then ignorant of biological and hormonal facts' (II 173). She heeds Frank's advice to her to leave her country for a while unless 'someone decided I should be in a mental hospital' (II 163). The trip to Europe is both cathartic and therapeutic but also creative.

At the end of the second volume, Frame is about to embark on a long journey to Europe: to London first or 'home', as her father surprisingly calls Great Britain for fear of appearing different in the family's eyes: 'I was startled. I had never heard him call the northern hemisphere *home*; he had usually laughed at people who still talked of the United Kingdom as *Home*; [...] I realized suddenly that my father's use of the word 'home' was [...] a dislike of appearing different' (II 188–9; author's italics). Like daughter, like father. However personal and specific the reasons for travelling abroad may be, they are also the reflection of the quest of a post-colonial writer, which makes Frame's relation to post-colonialism not such a simple issue: 'there is a special post-colonial crisis of identity [which is] the concern with the developement or recovery of an effective identifying relationship between self and place'.[22] The trip also answers a need of old: as a child, Frame used to be fascinated by the lexis of travelling – 'adventure', 'destination' – that so to speak 'performed' the journeys that could never take place because she was too poor. When she had to write a composition about a trip she had not made, Frame discovered the power of an imagination she would always cherish: 'realizing that to have an adventure, I did not need to travel in the lost Lizzie Ford, getting sick on the way, to beaches and rivers – I could experience an adventure by reading a book' (I 41). Fiction might be more interesting than life.

It is significant that the three volumes of the Autobiography should all end on a departure: the first one is 'zeugmatic':[23] '*I travelled south on the Sunday slow train to Dunedin and my Future*' (I 173, JF's italics), when Frame leaves family and home to go to university. The second ends on a departure on a larger scale, which Frame 'mythifies': 'like a mythical character about to embark on a long voyage' (II 187). She has become the 'niece who is going overseas', a new and more flattering label than the former 'mad niece' (II 189).

THE ENVOY FROM MIRROR CITY OR 'PORTRAIT OF THE ARTIST AS A YOUNG WOMAN'

Janet Frame's temporary exile is both a personal and historical necessity: she reiterates the quest of the Pakehas together with a personal quest for self-identity. And it is this identifying relationship Janet Frame is desperately looking for.

The interminable and sickening boat trip that takes Janet

'home' gives the measure of the distance that separates one home from the other. On her arrival in London, where she discovers that her letter of reservation has not reached its destination (another of her childhood fetish words) she uses New Zealand as a magical (though inefficient) password: *'all the way from New Zealand'* (III 18) as if the italics were meant to increase the distance and as if the effort implied by the trip deserved its natural reward. Whereas in her country, she had been the prestigious traveller, here, in London, she claims the prestige of the foreigner. The obstinate emphasis on New Zealand is an attempt at reterritorialization for one who has lost (or not yet found) her bearings. Ironically enough, her country becomes the refuge it has never been while she was living there. Frame is illustrating the psychological process that idealizes temporal and geographical distance. She clings to her luggage as a child clings to its mother also because it is the link, the umbilical cord, with the mother country. When she leaves her luggage in Paris because of a misunderstanding, she feels lost and almost amputated. The arrival in London appears as a real anticlimax. The woman at the hotel is the messenger of the bad news: 'Your letter didn't reach us' (III 18). Frame seems doomed to reproduce the 'universal drama of arrival'[24] that hinges upon a missing letter inducing a literalization of the preceding 'homelessness of self' that almost becomes a 'selflessness of self' as it means the loss of personal landmarks in a place that is obviously not the home her father had predicted it would be. The Edenic London Frame had imagined before her departure turns into a real Dickensian Hell of inhospitality (everything is bleak, dark and dreary). It is another of those Hells she has become accustomed to, be they the psychiatric hospitals or even less terrifying places. But even in this new Hell, Janet Frame does not seem to belong: 'I don't know where to stay' (III 18) she confesses to the woman at the hotel, in an echo to her desperate realization when, as a child, she did not dare to go back home after her punishment at school and was left with no place. Hence the mention of New Zealand as 'home' in a self-delusive but necessary attempt at recreating the lost 'paradise' of the past. In fact the YMCA she ends up in cannot but remind her of Seacliff, as if she were forever trapped: 'Memory recurs, cripples. There is no relief from its pain' (*PM* 15). The YMCA is a faithful replica of the asylum with its rules: '*Please leave the bath as you would wish others to find it*' (III 19; author's italics). To sum up Deleuze and Guattari's analyses in *Mille Plateaux*,[25] the first function of language is to give orders, as is made obvious through the repetition of the word 'control' twice within two lines.

Under its harmless appearance, language is violence (to cite Jean-Jacques Lecercle's title).[26] Be it in hospital or at the hotel, institutional order prevails (the two words have the same Latin etymology, *hospitalis* meaning refuge or shelter). And it is through this kind of occasional description that Frame gives the reader access to what she has been through in hospital, resorting to paralepsis as one of her favourite linguistic weapons to suggest a reality she cannot bear to face or relate directly, 'without the noise, without the constant jingling of keys and the attempt to control the guests' (III 19). The truth about the psychiatric hospital emerges when least expected. The letters the woman at the hostel (a figure of Cerberus at the gates of Hell) distributes become like 'holy tablets' that are all the holier as they are all the rarer, the qualifier 'holy' pertaining both to the mystical and to the mythical. According to Simon Petch in his article on 'Janet Frame and the Languages of Autobiography', 'Myth-making is an imaginative process that is central to Frame's writing of herself',[27] an analysis that corroborates Frame's own epigraph to the first volume: 'where the starting-point is myth'.

However, as usual with Frame, the disastrous arrival is transformed into a magic discovery rendered through the eloquent redeeming oxymoron: 'the fictional gift of the loss' (III 19), as if only fiction had the power to save one who has nothing. It is towards myth and intertextuality that Frame turns to discover another more promising, more beautiful world, 'that world' as she baptizes it, the place where she wants to live. The whole passage of the disastrous arrival is framed in by a hostile reality but the missing letter also provides Frame with the opportunity of a fictional flight into the world of letters together with the epiphanic discovery of the metaphoric Mirror City, first in its pluralized form before it becomes the title of the third volume, in its singular form. The fictional flight is narrated in the past (as opposed to the dialogue with the woman at the hotel) recomposed by the narrator as if to underline the contrast between fiction and reality. Frame's personal experience, however painful, opens for her the gates of the world of myth, to the point that she herself becomes myth: 'the ore of the polished fiction' (III 19). Thanks to this traumatizing arrival, she is born afresh. Reality sends her back to the world of fiction. Surrounded by her cumbersome though cherished luggage, she experiences an epiphanic mental journey that proves far richer and more beautiful than the real one she has just made. Frame plays the scenario of the perennial drama of arrival, perceiving herself as a heroine of fiction: graphy and autobiography become intertwined. Autobiography can be established through the remembrance of literary texts. The literary epiphany she experiences tears her away from the pain and the loss to transport her toward a blessed elsewhere – the gift. The missing letter has opened for her the world of letters. Through this experience, as throughout all the last volume, Frame theorizes the relation between fiction and reality, analysing the movement from one to the other, and the possible supremacy of one over the other. Her personal experience plunges her back into the world of fiction and its missing or stolen letters so that the personal anecdote acquires the status of a fictional topos, for example through Shakespeare. Thanks to literature to which she owes her life, the loss turns into the gift, the bane into a boon. The situation is no more irreversible than the diagnosis of schizophrenia, and creation finds its inspiration in difficulty. Her pain is absorbed and transcended by 'the fictional possibilities and enthusiasms' (III 19). Frame revisits Plato's myth since for her the reflection is superior to the original object, an intuition that will find its consecration in Ibiza. Frame is gradually becoming the artist she has always wanted to be, finding in personal experience the 'ore of the polished fiction'. 'The world of reading and the world of living' (I 54) are indeed linked as she had discovered on reading Grimm's *Fairy-Tales* for the first time. The very short stay in Paris is just as disastrous as the arrival in London, as Frame does not master the French language and leaves her luggage at the left luggage department, proving once more, if need be, that her life is in the power of words. The only positive memory she has of Paris is the recitation of some well-known lines – an experience that will be renewed in Ibiza – as if the only comfort she could find in foreign places was in the recognition of known places or words, a familiarity in an otherwise strange world.

The stay in Ibiza is ample illustration of the phenomenon. If Frame feels at ease almost immediately on this island, it is precisely because it is an island, a miniaturized version of her native land where she experiences a sort of spatial and temporal collapse: 'as if this land were mine and I had known it long ago' (III 68). She embarks upon a quest for lost places. The discovery of new places is in fact a rediscovery and this is what Janet Frame is looking for: trying to recreate home away from home, in the ambiguous feeling of one who has been unhappy at home, but nonetheless needs it, especially when away. Like the island which Janet experiences as an ambivalent motherland, the two Spanish women, her hostesses, play the parts of surrogate mothers. Even if – or maybe because – she does not master Spanish, she is quickly adopted into her new family to the point that she dreads speaking her own native language that seems out of place, like her luggage that finally arrives but too late and seems out of place, too, as it is no longer wanted. Janet is rechristened Janetta, a miniaturized Janet, whose integration requires the abiding by all sorts of rules. The process of adoption is broken off when Janet meets the American Bernard with whom she has a love affair,[28] though the word 'love' might be inappropriate in this case. In fact Janet means to put an end to her belated virginity (she is 31) and this meeting appears like a rite of initiation necessary to complete her (re)construction as if it were part and parcel of the therapy. She is ready to fall in love with Bernard because the time is right. The rite of initiation also and expectedly hinges upon words. Eroticism is linked with aestheticism and Bernard seduces Janet because he is able to quote some poetry.[29]

However, and despite the need and satisfaction of having rid herself of her cumbersome virginity, Janet is aware, right from the start, that the love story is anything but a love story. Her acute lucidity, a quality she displays in all circumstances, enables her to be both observer of herself and actress at the same time, even before the writing of the Autobiography gives her the temporal distance from events recollected in tranquillity. When she meets Bernard, she breaks the well-established rules and puts an end to her process of integration: 'Now, I had joined Los Americanos. I was Bernard's woman' (III 84). 'La escritora' has become 'La diabla'. Addressing the reader in a half humorous, half ironical tone: 'Picture me by the "blue Mediterranean"' (III 77), she is aware she has 'moved into a permanent cliché' (III 82). That feeling is conveyed and reinforced by the lexis she uses: the word 'picture' refers to photography and the scene she describes is also a cliché – sea, sex and sun – ironically summed up in her own verdict of her love affair: 'enacting a cliché drawn from all *True Romance* magazines' (III 80; author's italics), the quasi oxymoron (*True Romance*) which also recalls the title of the magazine the Frames read as adolescents. Frame's determination to live her love/sex story does not deprive her of her analytical, artistic eye: 'I apply cosmetics to what may be already a corpse' (III 83). The worm is in the fruit and it needs only Bernard's final words to deal the story a fatal blow as when Janet taunts him with the following question: 'What if I do have a baby?' (III 85), his terrified answer is unambiguous. But it is as if Janet had expected it, almost wished or provoked it, to confirm her deep-rooted conviction: this was not a love story, but only a step in the more general scheme of 'broadening her experience'. The end of the experience triggers her departure, which seems necessary to the preservation of Ibiza as a beautiful memory that might be spoilt if she stayed on. Songs of experience are songs of pain.

In Andorra, the following stage in her trip, she is faced with the choice of living 'a normal life' (an echo to the question she was asked in hospital before the lobotomy: 'Wouldn't you like to be normal?', II 107) with El Vici Mario who proposes to her, or living the life of a writer, in a world of her own, in a word, between 'this' and 'that' world. What determines her choice is the refusal to act her most 'accustomed role', that of the 'no trouble at all girl', of the submissive patient, reduced to an 'identity-destroying third person', an alienating 'non-person' (as the linguist Benveniste calls this impersonal third person), unable (or supposed not to be able) to make her own decisions. What El Vici offers her is the life of 'an uprooted "English-woman" going to live in the "colonies"' (III 98), an eloquent ironical reversal where she pictures herself as the colonizer among the poor peasants, once again 'actualizing' the link between self and country. Her longings are elsewhere, and not in the vineyards of the south of France where she would be picking grapes surrounded by a horde of children. Her choice is Mirror City, the realm of the happy few, of the artists whose difference is not stigmatized as it is for the mad, but glorified. Frame's shyness verges on aloofness, her 'princess among the scullions' stance.

The second stay in London – she seems to be retracing her steps – consecrates her as a writer. It is there that she writes several of her novels: *Faces in the Water*, *The Edge of the Alphabet*, *Uncle Pylades*,[30] *Scented Gardens for the Blind* and *The Adaptable Man*. But maybe even more importantly, it is in London, at the Maudsley Hospital, that she learns she has never suffered from schizophrenia (which she says she has always known). The news, however, comes as a shock for someone who had been wearing her illness like a second skin, and who had used it as an ally in her artistic creation. She no longer has her schizophrenia to turn to in times of trouble. The question the reader can ask him/herself (without expecting any answer) is about the role the illness has played in her writing, especially if she was not really ill, which makes it even more complex. How can she/we reconcile the fact that she is convinced she has never been ill with the fact that, as she keeps repeating, the illness had become a sort of ally? Frame seems once more to be 'leading the reader up the garden path', an impression that is reinforced when she declares, at the end of the third volume: 'I've created "selves"; but I've never written of "me" Why? Because if I make that hazardous journey to the Mirror City where everything I have known or seen or dreamed of is bathed in the light of another world, what use is there in returning only with a mirrorful of me?' (III 154), which is all the more puzzling as she had also declared in an interview: 'This is me which comes out'[31] while also negating the difference between fiction and autobiography: 'I look at everything from the point of view of fiction, and so it wasn't a change to be writing autobiography except the autobiography was more restrictive because it was based in fact, and I wanted to make an honest record of my life. But I was still bound by the choice of words and the shaping of the book, and that is similar to when one is writing fiction'.[32]

The reader of an autobiography may be entitled to expect 'the whole truth' (to quote Gisèle Mathieu-Castellani again) but it is as if Frame were refusing to make us this gift, as if she were cheating us. So what kind of autobiography has she written or why did she write one in the first place if she does not trust a genre that has almost destroyed her? Could this mean that this 'me' is elusive and by protecting it with inverted commas, she hints at the impossibility of finding it, knowing it and fixing it, which is not specific to her, but which seems to deny any autobiographical enterprise the capacity to do so? Her insistence on the various nicknames she was given as a child – Nini, Jean, Fuzzy – aims at enhancing this sense of diversity or fragmentation. Frame's aim is to find her own identity, instead of being thrown into the passive role of the child or the patient. And, as we have seen, it is through writing and travelling – that is through geo/graphy – that she will, the second being an incentive to the first. 'There is no 'pure' autobiography' (I 161) she also declared, meaning that autobiography is always and inevitably a generic mixture, without relinquishing the project to write one as a keystone to all her works, since it is her last work but one.

At the end of volume III, the decision to go back 'home' is (once more) made for her when her father's death demands that she should return. But if this is the official reason, her own analysis contradicts it. She refuses to be a writer in exile because she adheres to Frank Sargeson's conviction that there is no place like home. This volume, like the two preceding ones, ends on a departure, or rather a return: 'The Return of the Native' or of the prodigal Janet. But she goes back a famous writer and no longer as the 'mad' person.

She has looped the loop: 'The path that leads from the outer to the inner self goes round the world',[33] a statement that can be taken literally in Frame's case. Her difference has been recognized as the valuable, prestigious kind of difference, relegating to the past the shameful, invalidating, unacceptable one. Not only has she become a famous writer, she also presents herself as a literary pioneer, once more stressing the link between creation and geography (which the title of volume III confirms): writing gives access to special new privileged territories she is willing to show to her followers.

Frame has no doubt contributed to inscribe her country on the world's literary map, even if this country almost destroyed her. It is as if she were taking a spectacular revenge, proving to the world, and to New Zealand in particular, that it would have been sheer madness to lobotomize her.

Notes

1. INTRODUCTION

1. Gina Mercer, *Janet Frame, Subversive Fictions* (Dunedin: University of Otago Press, 1994).
2. Philippe Lejeune, *Le pacte autobiographique* (Paris: Seuil, 1975).
3. Jean-Pierre Miraux, *L'Autobiographie* (Paris: Nathan, 1996).
4. Jean-Jacques Lecercle, 'Folie et Littérature: De Foucault à Janet Frame', *La Licorne*, (Poitiers: Presses Universitaires de Poitiers, 2001), 30.
5. Judith Butler, *Bodies that Matter* (New York and London: Routledge, 1993).
6. Brigitte Barry, 'Histoire d'une Vie, Vie d'une Histoire: figures autobiographiques chez Janet Frame', *Confluences XIII, Ecrits et Figures* (Nanterre: Publidix, 1996), 13–28 (my translation).

CHAPTER 2. THE AUTOBIOGRAPHICAL NOVELS

1. Simone Oettli-van Delden, *Surfaces of Strangeness: Janet Frame and the Rhetoric of Madness* (Wellington: Victoria University Press, 2003), 105.
2. Ibid. 112.
3. Ibid. 113.
4. Karin Hansson, *The Unstable Manifold: Janet Frame's Challenge to Determinism* (Lund: Lund University Press, 1996), 71.
5. W. D. Ashcroft, 'Beyond the Alphabet: *Owls Do Cry*', in Jeanne Delbaere (ed), *The Ring Of Fire, Essays on Janet Frame* (Sydney: Dangarro Press, 1992), 71.
6. Elizabeth Alley, '"An Honest Record": An Interview with Janet Frame', Landfall, 45.2 (1991), 161.
7. Oettli-van Delden, *Surfaces of Strangeness*, 104.
8. Ashcroft, 'Beyond the Alphabet', 70.
9. Oettli-van Delden, *Surfaces of Strangeness*, 113.
10. Alley, 'An Honest Record', 155.

11. Emile Benveniste, *Problèmes de Linguistique Générale* (Paris: Gallimard, 1966).
12. Oettli-van Delden, *Surfaces of Strangeness*, 114.
13. Ibid. 179, n. 78.
14. J. A. Cuddon, *The Penguin Dictionary of Literary Terms and Literary Theory* (Harmondsworth: Penguin, 1977), 43.
15. Alice Braun, *Janet Frame: le féminin et la marge*, doctoral thesis, Nanterre University, December 2008, 223.
16. Christine Favier, '"Where too many mouths are locked" ou Janet Frame et le refus d'une voix dominante', unpublished article, 2 (my translation).
17. Oscar Wilde, *The Picture of Dorian Gray* (1891) (New York and London: Norton Critical Edition, 1987), 149.
18. Oettli-van Delden, *Surfaces of Strangeness*, 115–16.
19. Claude Burgelin, 'L'autobiographie, genre métis' in Philippe Lejeune (ed), *L'autobiographie en procès* (Nanterre: Publidix, 1997) (my translation).
20. Oettli-van Delden, *Surfaces of Strangeness*, 116.
21. Alley, 'An Honest Record', 155.
22. Michel Foucault, *Surveiller et Punir* (Paris: Gallimard, 1975).
23. Marianne Camus 'Faces in the Water de Janet Frame: Le monde des fous ou un monde de fous?', *Frontières et syncrétisme* 61 (Université de Franche-Comtés 2002), 62–74.
24. Braun, *Janet Frame*, 32 (my translation).
25. Ibid. 44.
26. Monika Reif-Hülser, '"Glass Beads of Fantasy" Janet Frame's *Faces in the Water*, or: The Enigma of Identity', *REAL: Yearbook of Research in English and American Literature* 12 (1996), 200, in Braun, *Janet Frame*, 215.
27. Jeremy Bentham, *Panopticon: Or The Inspection House* (1791), and Michel Foucault, *Surveiller et Punir* (Paris: Gallimard, 1975). A panopticon is a circular building with an observation tower in the centre in an open space surrounded by an outer wall made up of cells for the incarceration of mental patients or convicts. The purpose of the design is to increase the security through the effectiveness of the surveillance. Source: Wikipedia.
28. Tonya Blowers, *Locating the Self: Re-reading Autobiography as Theory and Practice, with particular reference to the writings of Janet Frame*, PhD thesis, University of Warwick, 1998, 87.
29. Camus, 'Faces in the Water', 71 (my translation).
30. Claire Bazin, 'Taboo or Not Taboo? Janet Frame's Autobiography', 24.2 (*Commonwealth Essays and Studies*: Presses de l'Université de Bourgogne, 2002), 17–27.
31. Le Breton in Ivane Mortelette, '"Burgled of Body": corps et identité

chez Janet Frame' in Claire Bazin and Marie-Claude Perrin-Chenour (eds), *Textes et Genres, L'écriture du corps dans la littérature féminine de langue anglaise*, Actes des colloques de Juin 2005 et Juin 2006 (Nanterre: Publidix, 2007), 123–34.
32. Elaine Showalter, *The Female Malady: Women, Madness and English Culture, 1830–1980* (London: Virago, 1987), 40.
33. Oettli-van Delden, *Surfaces of Strangeness*, 129.

CHAPTER 3. 'THE HOUSE OF FICTION' (*SF* 233)

1. Karin Hansson, *The Unstable Manifold: Janet Frame's Challenge to Determinism* (Lund: Lund University Press, 1996), 6.
2. Ibid. 73.
3. Jan Cronin, 'The Theoretical Terrain of the Text: Reading Frame through *The Edge of the Alphabet*', *Journal of New Zealand Studies* No. 2/3, October (2003–2004), 45–63.
4. Ibid. 15.
5. Ibid. 14.
6. Susan Ash, 'Janet Frame: The Female Artist as Hero', *Journal of New Zealand Literature* 6 (1988), 170–89.
7. Alice Braun, '*A State of Siege*: Le langage du trou', in Claire Bazin and Marie-Claude Perrin-Chenour, *Textes et Genres, L'écriture du corps dans la littérature féminine de langue anglaise*, Actes des colloques de Juin 2005 et Juin 2006 (Nanterre: Publidix, 2007), 113–22.
8. Alex Calder's, for example, 'The Closure of Sense: Janet Frame, Language and the Body', *Antic* 3 (1987), 93–103.
9. Cronin, '"Encircling Tubes of Being": New Zealand as Hypothetical Site in Janet Frame's *A State of Siege* (1966)', *Journal of New Zealand Literature* 23.2 (2005), 79–91, 9.
10. Simone Oettli-van Delden, *Surfaces of Strangeness: Janet Frame and the Rhetoric of Madness* (Wellington: Victoria University Press, 2003), 129.
11. Jeanne Delbaere, 'Beyond the Word: *Scented Gardens for the Blind*' in Jeanne Delbaere (ed), *The Ring of Fire: Essays on Janet Frame* (Sydney: Dangarro Pres, 1992), 103.
12. Ibid. 100.
13. Oettli-van Delden, *Surfaces of Strangeness*, 132.
14. Delbaere, 'Beyond the Word' in Delbaere (ed), *The Ring of Fire*, 108.
15. Quoted in Hansson, *The Unstable Manifold*, 41.
16. Victor Dupont, 'Janet Frame's Brave New World: *Intensive Care*' in Delbaere (ed), *The Ring of Fire*, 149–60.
17. J. Delbaere, 'Turnlung in the Noon Sun: An Analysis of *Daughter Buffalo*', in Delbaere (ed), *Ring of Fire*, 168.
18. Ibid. 169.

19. Ibid. 161.
20. Christine Favier, '*Daughter Buffalo*: deux narrateurs, trois narrateurs, ou un seul?', unpublished article, 7–8, my translation.
21. Judith Dell Panny, 'Opposite and Adjacent to the Postmodern in *Living in the Maniototo*' in Delbaere (ed), *Ring of Fire*, 193.
22. Ibid. 189.
23. Ibid. 188.
24. Dorothy Jones, 'The Hawk of Language and the Plain of Blood: *Living in the Maniototo*', in Delbaere (ed), *Ring of Fire*, 177.
25. Dell Panny, 'Opposite and Adjacent', 196.
26. Ibid. 194.
27. Jones, 'Hawk of Language', 180.
28. Elizabeth Alley, '"An Honest Record", An Interview with Janet Frame', *Landfall* 45.2 (1991), 165.
29. Jeanne Delbaere: '*The Carpathians*: Memory and Survival in the Global Village' in Delbaere (ed), *Ring of Fire*, 199–208.
30. Marc Delrez, 'Boundaries and Beyond: Memory as Quest in *The Carpathians*', in Delbaere (ed), *Ring of Fire*, 215.
31. Ibid. 216.
32. Ibid. 217.
33. Michele Leggott in Michael King, *Wrestling With The Angel: A Life of Janet Frame* (Harmondsworth: Penguin, 2000), 488.
34. Delbaere, '*The Carpathians*' in Delbaere (ed), *Ring of Fire*, 203.

CHAPTER 4. SHORT STORIES AND POEMS: GENERIC VARIETY

1. Claire Bazin, 'Janet Frame: "Keel and Kool" or Autobiogra/fiction?' In *Commonwealth Essays and Studies*, 29.2 (Spring 2007), 19–28.
2. Claire Bazin, 'Taboo or not Taboo? Janet Frame's Autobiography', *Commonwealth Essays and Studies* 24.2 (Spring 2002), 17–27.
3. Hélène Cixous, 'Sorties: Out & Out: Attacks/Ways Out/Forays' in Hélène Cixous and Catherine Clément, *The Newly Born Woman* (1975; Manchester: Manchester University Press, 1986), 70, quoted in Gina Mercer, *Janet Frame: Subversive Fictions* (Dunedin: University of Otago Press, 1994), 253.
4. Marc Delrez, 'The Unbearable Burden of Being "Snowman, Snowman"', *Commonwealth Essays and Studies* 17.1 (Autumn 1994), 89–99, 95.
5. Roger Robinson and Nelson Wattie, *The Oxford Companion to New Zealand Literature* (Melbourne: Oxford University Press, 1998).
6. Valérie Baisnée, 'A Home in Language, The (Meta)Physical World

of Janet Frame's Poetry' in Jan Cronin and Simone Drichel (eds), *Frameworks: Contemporary Criticism on Janet Frame* (Amsterdam and New York: Rodopi, 2009), 88–105.
7. In *The Oxford Companion to New Zealand Literature,* 188.
8. Baisnée, 'A Home in Language', 90.
9. Ibid. 101.
10. Ibid. 95.
11. Ibid.
12. Ibid. 97.
13. Ibid. 93.
14. Ibid. 105.
15. Marc Delrez, 'The Legacy of Invention: Determinism and metafiction in Janet Frame's *Mona Minim and the Smell of the Sun*', *Journal of Postcolonial Writing,* 45.1 (London: Routledge, March 2009).
16. Ibid. 29.
17. Ibid. 34.
18. *Remembrances of Things Past* (1913–27), Marcel Proust's most prominent work, is popularly known for its extended length and the notion of involuntary memory, the most famous example being the 'episode of the madeleine', which unlocks the narrator's past as the subject of his novel. Source: Wikipedia.
19. Alice Braun, '*A State of Siege*: Le langage du trou', in Claire Bazin and Marie-Claude Perrin-Chenour, *Textes et Genres, L'écriture du corps dans la littérature féminine de langue anglaise,* Actes des colloques de Juin 2005 et Juin 2006 (Nanterre: Publidix, 2007), 294.

CHAPTER 5. *AN ANGEL AT MY TABLE*

1. Elizabeth Alley, '"An Honest Record": An Interview with Janet Frame', *Landfall* 45.2 (1991), 155.
2. Goethe, *The Sorrows of Young Werther* (1774) (New York: Modern Library, 2005).
3. Gisèle Mathieu-Castellani, *La Scène Judiciaire de l'Autobiographie* (Paris: PUF), 1996.
4. Jean-Paul Sartre, *Les Mots* (Paris: Gallimard, 1964, my translation).
5. In Karin Hansson, *The Unstable Manifold: Janet Frame's Challenge to Determinism* (Lund: Lund University Press), 5.
6. Claire Bazin, 'Un monde de mots dans *To the Is-land*', *Confluences* 12 (Nanterre: Publidix, 1996), 137–48 (my translation).
7. Alley, 'An Honest Record', 156.
8. Judith Dell Panny, in Elizabeth Alley (ed), *The Inward Sun, Celebrating the Life and Work of Janet Frame* (Wellington: Daphne Basell, 1994), 146.

9. Tonya Blowers, *Locating the Self: Re-reading Autobiography as Theory and Practice, with Particular Reference to the Writings of Janet Frame*, PhD thesis, University of Warwick, 1998, 80.
10. Ibid. 77.
11. Philippe Lejeune, *Le pacte autobiographique* (Paris: Seuil, 1975), 34 (my translation).
12. Alley, 'An Honest Record', 158.
13. Blowers, *Locating the Self*, 87.
14. Michel Foucault, *Histoire de la folie à l'âge classique* (Paris: Gallimard, 1972).
15. Claire Bazin, '"Homelessness of Self": Janet Frame's Autobiography' in Frédéric Regard and Geoffrey Wall (eds): *Mapping the Self: Space, Identity, Discourse in British Auto/Biography* (Saint Etienne: Presses de l'Université de Saint-Etienne, 2003), 313–21.
16. Paralipsis is a kind of irony in which the speaker proposes not to speak of a matter, but still somehow reveals it. Example: 'I know who did it, but I won't mention Bill's name'. Source: Internet.
17. Claude Burgelin, in Philippe Lejeune (ed) *L'Autobiographie en Procès* (Nanterre: Publidix, 1997), 54 (my translation).
18. André Breton in Robert Escarpit, *L'Humour, Que Sais-Je?* (Paris: PUF, 1960), 70, my translation.
19. Roland Barthes, *La Chambre Claire, Note sur la photographie* (Paris: Gallimard, Seuil, 1980) and Susan Sontag, *On Photography* (New York: Farrar, Straus and Giroux, 1977).
20. Georges Gusdorf, *Les Ecritures du moi* (Paris: Odile Jacob, 1991), 8 (my translation).
21. New Zealand novelist, short story writer, nonfiction writer, and dramatist. Sargeson's fiction focuses on alienation and isolation among New Zealand's lower classes. His characters are often uneducated, inarticulate and frustrated male drifters and deviants who cannot conform to the standards and expectations of society. Source: Google/Criticism. The hut was in Takapuna. Takapuna is a central, coastal suburb of North Shore City, located in the northern North Island of New Zealand.
22. B. Ashcroft, G. Griffiths, H.Tiffin, *The Empire Writes Back: Theory and Practice in Post-Colonial Literatures* (London: Routledge, 1989), 8–9.
23. 'Zeugma' in Greek means 'yoking'; 'in the most common present usage, it is applied to expressions in which a single word stands in the same grammatical relation to two or more other words, but with some alteration in its meaning from one instance to the next' in M. H. Abrams, *A Glossary of Literary Terms* (1957; New York: Holt Rinehart & Winston, 1971 (updated Dan S. Norton and Peter Rushton).
24. Claire Bazin, 'Une seule lettre vous manque dans *An Angel at My*

Table' in *Les Ecrivains en Voyage* (Angers: CIRHILL, 2004), 311–23, 313.
25. Gilles Deleuze and Félix Guattari, *Capitalisme et Schizophénie, tome 2: Mille Plateaux* (Paris: Editions de Minuit, 1980).
26. Jean-Jacques Lecercle, *The Violence of Language* (London and New York: Routledge, 1990).
27. Simon Petch: 'Janet Frame and the Languages of Autobiography', *Australian and New Zealand Studies in Canada* 5 (1991), 58–71, 61.
28. Bernard is a fictional name for George Parlette, 'a thirty-year old accountant [...] who had left a wife and two children' in Michael King, *Wrestling With The Angel: a life of Janet Frame* (Harmondsworth Penguin, 2000), 164.
29. Claire Bazin, 'Sea, Sex and Sun: Janet Frame's Experiences in Ibiza', New Zealand Conference, Florence 2008, to be published.
30. In King, *Wrestling With The Angel*, 540, n. 29: 'Frame never offered this manuscript for publication and, when asked, declined to outline its content and themes'.
31. Alley, 'An Honest Record', 158.
32. Ibid. 161.
33. Georges Gusdorf, *Les Ecritures du moi*, 8, my translation. (Paris: Odile Jacob, 1991).

Select Bibliography

WORKS BY JANET FRAME

The Lagoon and Other Stories (London: Bloomsbury (1951); Flamingo, 1993).
Owls Do Cry (London: The Women's Press (1961); 1996).
Faces in the Water (1961) (London: The Women's Press, 1980).
The Edge of the Alphabet (1962) (New York: George Braziller, 1995).
The Reservoir: Stories and Sketches (1963) (New York: George Braziller, 1993).
Scented Gardens for the Blind (1964) (London: The Women's Press, 1982).
The Adaptable Man (1965) (New York: George Braziller, 1992).
A State of Siege (1966) (New York: George Braziller, 1980).
The Pocket Mirror (1967) (London: The Women's Press, 1992).
Yellow Flowers in the Antipodean Room (*The Rainbirds*) (1969) (New York: George Braziller, 1994).
Mona Minim and the Smell of the Sun (1969) (London, Bloomsbury Classics, 1993).
Intensive Care (1970) (Wellington, Auckland, Sydney, Melbourne: Reed, 1971).
Daughter Buffalo (New York: George Braziller, 1972; Flamingo, 1993).
Living in the Maniototo (1979) (London: The Women's Press, 1981).
You Are Now Entering the Human Heart (1983) (London: The Women's Press, 1984).
To The Is-Land (1983) (London: Paladin, 1987); *An Angel at My Table* (1984) (London: Paladin, 1987); *The Envoy from Mirror City* (1985) (London: Paladin, 1987).
The Carpathians (1988) (London: Flamingo, 1993).
The Complete Autobiography (London: The Women's Press, 1990).
The Goose Bath (Auckland: Random House, 2006).
Towards Another Summer (Auckland: Random House, 2007).

CRITICAL WORKS

Alley, Elizabeth (ed), *The Inward Sun: Celebrating the Life and Work of Janet Frame* (Wellington: Daphne Brasell Association Press, 1994). A collection of essays privileging personal responses from famous writers and friends to Janet Frame and her work.

Baisnée, Valérie, *Gendered Resistance: The Autobiographies of Simone de Beauvoir, Maya Angelou, Janet Frame and Marguerite Duras* (Amsterdam: Rodopi, 1997). A percipient comparative scrutiny based on various critical approaches.

Bazin, Claire and Braun, Alice, *Janet Frame, The Lagoon and other Stories: Naissance d'une Oeuvre* (Paris: PUF, 2010). A study of the short stories.

Blowers, Tonya, *Locating the Self: Re-reading Autobiography as Theory and Practice, with Particular Reference to the Writings of Janet Frame*, PhD thesis, University of Warwick, 1998. An excellent PhD.

Cronin J. and S. Drichel (eds), *Frameworks* (Amsterdam and New York: Rodopi, 2009). The collection offers new perspectives on Frame studies, and examines the relationship between her work and its critical context.

Delbaere, Jeanne (ed), *The Ring of Fire: Essays on Janet Frame* (Sydney: Dangaroo Press, 1992). A collection of articles on most of Frame's novels. Delbaere's on *Scented Gardens for the Blind* and *Daughter Buffalo* and Delrez's on *The Carpathians* are excellent.

Delrez, Marc, *Manifold Utopia: The Novels of Janet Frame* (Amsterdam: Rodopi, 2002). The most detailed and convincing study of Frame's novels to this day. Both highly sophisticated and readable.

Hansson, Karin, *The Unstable Manifold: Janet Frame's Challenge to Determinism* (Lund: Lund University Press, 1996). Frame's novels in the light of (anti) Darwinism: a very interesting if sometimes questionable study.

King, Michael, *Wrestling With The Angel: a life of Janet Frame* (Harmondsworth: Penguin, 2000). An excellent, very complete and highly readable work.

Mercer, Gina, *Janet Frame: Subversive Fictions* (Dunedin: University of Otago Press, 1994). A very complete study of the novels and the autobiographies from a feminist perspective.

Oettli-van Delden, Simone, *Surfaces of Strangeness: Janet Frame and the Rhetoric of Madness* (Wellington: Victoria University Press, 2003). A study of the exploration and expression of madness in Frame's novels and Autobiography.

ARTICLES

Alley, Elizabeth, '"An Honest Record": An Interview with Janet Frame', *Landfall* 45.2 (1991), 154–68.

Ash, Susan, '"The Absolute, Distanced Image": Janet Frame's Autobiography' *Journal of New Zealand Literature* 11 (1993), 21–40. A seminal essay on Frame's autobiographical postures.

Baisnée, Valérie, 'A Home in Language – The (Meta)Physical World of Janet Frame's Poetry', in Cronin and Drichel (eds), *Frameworks*. A very good and useful chapter on this neglected part of Frame's work.

Bazin, Claire, 'Taboo or Not Taboo? Janet Frame's Autobiography', *Commonwealth Essays and Studies* 24.2 (2002), 17–27. A study of taboo topics and Frame's emancipation from them through writing.

———, '"Homelessness of Self": Janet Frame's Autobiography' in Regard, Frédéric and Wall, Geoffrey (eds), *Mapping the Self: Space, Identity, Discourse in British Auto/Biography* (Saint Etienne: Presses de l'Université de Saint-Etienne, 2003), 313–21. The article focuses on the acute sense of place in Frame's work, from a personal and historical point of view.

———, "From the Rim of the Farthest Circle", *Journal of New Zealand Literature* 24.1 (2006), 115–29. An analysis of all the forms of exclusion Frame had to deal with.

———, 'Janet Frame: "Keel and Kool" or Autobiogra/fiction', *Commonwealth Essays and Studies* 29.2 (Spring 2007), 19–28. The study is based on the links with the Autobiography, on the role of clichés and on photography.

Blowers, Tonya, 'Madness, Philosophy and Literature: A Reading of Janet Frame's *Faces in the Water*', *Journal of New Zealand Literature* 14 (1996) 74–89. An excellent comparative analysis of the construction of madness.

Braun, Alice, 'The Author at Work: Two Short Stories by Janet Frame', *Commonwealth* 30.1 (2007), 93–103. A thorough, comparative study of 'Jan Godfrey' and 'Flu and Eye Trouble'.

Cronin, Jan, 'The Theoretical Terrain of the Text: Reading Frame through The Edge of the Alphabet', *Journal of New Zealand Studies* 2.3 (October 2003–October 2004) (2005), 45–63. A highly theoretical, verging-on-the-obscure, article.

———, '"Encircling Tubes of Being": New Zealand as Hypothetical Site in Janet Frame's *A State of Siege* (1966)', *Journal of New Zealand Literature* 23.2 (2005), 79–91. Very theoretical, though more readable than the preceding one.

Delrez, Marc, '"Boundaries and Beyond": Memory as Quest in Janet

Frame's *The Carpathians*', *Commonwealth* 13.1 (1990), 95–105.

———, 'The Unbearable Burden of Being "Snowman, Snowman"', *Commonwealth* 17.1 (1994), 89–99. These two articles are just as fascinating as the book.

———, 'The Legacy of Invention: Determinism and Metafiction in Janet Frame's *Mona Minim and the Smell of the Sun*', *Journal of Postcolonial Writing* 45 (March 2009). A brilliant study of the story.

Lecercle, Jean-Jacques 'Folie et littérature: de Foucault à Frame', Poitiers: *La Licorne* 55 (2000), 293–304. An analysis of Frame's writing before and after the diagnosis.

Mortelette, Ivane, '"A Proof that I Did Exist": Janet Frame and Photography', *Journal of New Zealand Literature* 24.1 (2006), 94–114. A very convincing article on the importance of photography in Frame's work.

Petch, Simon, 'Janet Frame and the Languages of Autobiography', *Australian and New Zealand Literature in Canada* 5 (1991), http://web.archive.org/web/20000416093840/www.arts.uwo.ca/~andrewf/anzsc/anzsccont.htm. An extremely useful account of Frame's Autobiography and autobiographical writing.

Index

Alley, Elizabeth, 111–17, 119
Ash, Susan, 35, 113, 120
Ashcroft, Bill, 10, 111, 116
autobiography, 28, 88, 92, 111, 112, 115, 116, 119

Baisnée, Valérie, 75, 115, 120
Bazin, Claire, 112–17, 120
Blowers, Tonya, 112, 116, 119, 120
Braun, Alice, 15, 21, 31, 36, 86, 112, 113, 115, 120

Campion, Jane, 1, 4
cliché, 8, 14, 23, 35, 37, 42–4, 56, 66, 67, 69, 80, 89, 90, 100, 101
Cronin, Jan, 29, 32, 37, 113, 115, 119, 120

Delbaere, Jane, 38, 42, 50, 55, 111, 113, 114, 119
Delrez, Marc, 1, 32–4, 37–9, 47–50, 57, 64, 81, 114, 115, 119, 120
Dunedin, 42, 45, 80, 103, 111, 114, 119

feminist, 2, 3, 71, 119
Frame, Janet,
    The Adaptable Man, 28, 35, 46–9, 53, 54, 109, 118

An Angel at My Table, 1, 88–110, 115, 117, 118
The Carpathians, 31, 37, 39, 42, 56, 61–4, 82, 83, 114, 118–20
Daughter Buffalo, 29, 42, 44, 46, 53–7, 86, 114, 118, 119
The Edge of the Alphabet, 7, 15, 28, 29–33, 34, 38, 109, 113, 118, 120
Faces in the Water, 17–27, 18, 24, 25, 27, 41, 50, 57, 65, 71, 80, 96, 99, 109, 112, 118, 120
Intensive Care, 3, 6, 12, 28, 31, 34, 46, 49–53, 55, 59, 60, 69, 75–7, 79, 83, 86, 113, 118
The Lagoon, 2, 65–74, 100, 118
Living in the Maniototo, 24, 29, 30, 43, 50, 52, 56, 57–61, 63, 71, 76, 95, 114, 118
Mona Minim and the Smell of the Sun, 72, 81–4, 115, 118, 121
Owls Do Cry, 6–17, 18, 19, 25, 26, 31–3, 35, 43, 50, 69, 71, 77, 91, 99, 111, 118

The Pocket Mirror, The Goose Bath, 75–80, 118
The Rainbirds, 14, 42–6, 60, 118
The Reservior, 2, 65–74, 102, 118
Scented Gardens for the Blind, 21, 28, 31, 38–42, 56, 63, 73, 81, 109, 113, 118, 119
A State of Siege, 28, 30, 32, 34–8, 48, 115, 118, 120
Towards Another Summer, 4, 28, 66, 75, 76, 78, 84–7, 118
You Are Now Entering the Human Heart, 65–74, 118

Gusdorf, Georges, 116, 117

Hansson, Karin, 28, 48, 49, 111, 113, 115, 119
home, 103, 104, 107, 110, 114, 115, 116, 120

Ibiza, 79, 95, 106–8

King, Michael, 2, 27, 31, 76, 85, 114, 117

language, 6–8, 14, 16, 20, 22, 29–31, 33, 37–9, 42, 53, 54, 59, 61, 63, 64, 66, 67, 72, 73, 74, 76, 80, 86, 90, 105–7, 113–15, 117, 120, 121
Lecercle, Jean-Jacques, 4, 105, 111, 117, 121
Lejeune, Philippe, 1, 7, 88, 111, 112, 116
London, 17, 31–3, 40, 49, 50, 60, 79, 93, 96, 102, 104, 106, 109

Mercer, Gina, 1, 6, 9, 11, 13, 21, 22, 25, 26, 29, 30, 40–2, 50, 58, 71, 99, 111, 114, 119
Mortelette, Ivane, 113, 121

Oamaru, 65, 86
Oettli van-Delden, Simone, 7, 16, 35, 38, 40, 101, 111, 112, 113, 119

Petch, Simon, 105, 117, 121

schizophrenia, 2, 40, 45, 93, 96, 97, 101, 102, 106, 109
society, 64, 67–73, 89, 99–101, 116
solitude, 13, 45, 66, 67, 70, 86

taboos, 53, 73, 89, 97

www.ingramcontent.com/pod-product-compliance
Lightning Source LLC
Chambersburg PA
CBHW030144240426
43672CB00005B/256